"Encouraging, honest, comforting, helpful. But most of all it draws you to the One who can give what others cannot. What a welcome resource to help give stability and peace."

—H. Norman Wright, licensed marriage therapist and award-winning and bestselling author of more than seventy books, including *Communication: Key to Your Marriage* and *Quiet Times for Couples*

"Kristin gives us a glimpse of the beauty that grew out of the ashes of her divorce. She has chosen beauty over bitterness. I applaud her faith-filled champion's heart."

—Jackie Kendall, bestselling coauthor of *Lady in Waiting* and president of Power to Grow Ministries

"Kristin is blessed to communicate spiritual truths with heart-transforming simplicity. Allow God's grace and mercy to unfold from these pages and restore your soul."

—Michelle Borquez, coauthor of *Live, Laugh, Love Again*

"Kristin Armstrong's book is a profoundly honest and intensely personal reflection."

—Tammy Maltby, cohost of four-time Emmy-nominated *Aspiring Women* and author of *Confessions of a Good Christian Girl* and *Lifegiving*

happily ever after

Walking with Peace and Courage
Through a Year of Divorce

Kristin Armstrong

FaithWords

New York Boston Nashville

happily ever after

FaithWords
Hachette Book Group
237 Park Avenue
New York, NY 10017

www.FaithWords.com

Printed in the United States of America

Originally published in hardcover by Hachette Book Group.

First Trade Edition: April 2008
10 9 8 7 6 5 4 3 2

FaithWords is a division of Hachette Book Group, Inc.
The FaithWords name and logo are trademarks of Hachette Book Group, Inc.

The publisher is not responsible for websites (or their content) that are not
owned by the publisher.

ISBN 978-0-446-50395-2 (pbk.)
Library of Congress Control Number: 2006930300

FOR MY CHILDREN

Luke, Grace, and Isabelle

INTRODUCTION

Circumstances in life often take us places that we never intended to go. We visit some places of beauty, others of pain and desolation. I never imagined that divorce would be part of my life history or my family's legacy. When people say that divorce can be more painful than death, I understand why. But like any great trial, God uses everything for good, if we allow Him to heal us. Every moment is teachable; every ounce of hurt can prune us for future happiness. I am sorry for your pain. I empathize with where your heart is if you are opening this book. I pray for your journey to wholeness, and I know the Lord can replace your loss with His love and your pain with His indescribable peace.

I have walked this path, from the trenches of despair, through pitfalls of anger, bottlenecks of blame, along the cliffs of loneliness and fear. I have felt the cold draft of my own sin and the warm embrace of forgiveness. In navigating my ups and downs, I found my unshakable compass in the Lord. If you can find yours more quickly, it will spare you a measure of anguish. That is part of my intention for writing this book.

My primary intention is gratitude. As my numbness subsided, I figured out that I had to purge the negative and pour in the positive—the Word of God. I kept a journal of all the Scripture that I held close, and the result is what I offer you in this book. I vowed when I got to the other side that I would not forget who carried me. This is my thank-you note to God.

May you find your center, a strength and courage you did not know you could summon. The terrain ahead is rough, but there are gifts hidden along your path of faith.

Blessings,

—*Kristin Armstrong*

happily ever after

AN END MARKS A NEW BEGINNING

This month is to be for you the first month,
the first month of your year.

EXODUS 12:2

This year will be epic for you—momentous in so many ways. You will see both ends of the spectrum of good days and bad days, and you will learn to treasure the simplicity and grace of middle ground.

As much as it may not feel like your year right now, maintain an open mind. The Lord is already at work behind the scenes, transforming your life and you. He is making you into the woman He had in mind when He created you. Prepare to continually be at a crossroad, as many choices are in front of you. Every day, many times a day, you will make decisions that determine the rest of your story. You can choose healing or resentment, freedom or unforgiveness, love or closure, joy or despair.

Each choice, made faithfully, leads to more choices. Eventually you will be surprised to find yourself healed, whole, and happily living your brand-new life. It's okay if you think that sounds crazy or impossible, because in 2003 I thought the same thing. God loves to laugh at the impossible, and soon enough, you'll be laughing too.

CHOOSING YOUR PATH

The fruit of righteousness will be peace;
the effect of righteousness
will be quietness and confidence forever.

ISAIAH 32:17

❧

The poet Robert Frost describes in his well-known poem "The Road Not Taken" two roads diverging in the woods and the timeless dilemma of choosing which path to take.

You are at this juncture. You stand on the threshold of a decision with implications of eternal magnitude. The road splits here—choose the path of righteousness and live in the light, or choose the path of rationalization and remain in the dark. It is imperative that you recognize the significance of a clean and complete healing and choose your path accordingly.

This choice not only affects you, but it can also shape the legacy you leave for your children and grandchildren. The path of sour bitterness, crusty resentment, and cold regret breeds generations of despair. The path of righteousness grants generations of peace, quietness, and confidence.

You won't find the right path by default; the choice is deliberate. Which path leads to the kind of life you desire for yourself and those you love? Choose wisely.

PERSEVERING WITH GOD

We are hard pressed on every side,
but not crushed;
perplexed, but not in despair;
persecuted, but not abandoned;
struck down, but not destroyed.

2 CORINTHIANS 4:8–9

"That which does not kill you only makes you stronger."

"God never gives you more than you can bear."

These are some worldly equivalents of the above Scripture from 2 Corinthians. When I first read those verses, I certainly felt pressed, perplexed, persecuted, abandoned, and struck down. I wanted to wallow in those feelings. I was angry at God. I had a very bad case of, "Why me?"

Why not me?

Throughout history, the strongest faith journeys have had seasons of pain and adversity. With Christ as our pinnacle example, we can say with confidence that it is impossible to be of great faith and not endure suffering. Hard times are inescapable. Now, how we react to hard times is indeed another matter. We can look away from God in anger and unbelief, and if we choose to remain this way, be crushed, in despair, abandoned, and destroyed. Or we can look to God, and know beyond our understanding that He is at the core of our testing, and that Jesus alone lights a path to the other side.

Calling All Control Freaks

*Trust in the Lord with all your heart and lean not on
your own understanding; in all your ways acknowledge
him, and he will make your paths straight.*

PROVERBS 3:5–6

❧

Now is not the time to make sense of this mess. You are too
tired, your perspective is too limited, and you don't have the
strength or the vision to do this on your own. The stronger
you are in worldly terms, the more difficult it is to submit
in spiritual terms. But really, what choice do you have?

Trust means letting go of your floundering attempts to
manipulate people, circumstances, or timing. It is a grand
release of control, returning the reins to the only One who
knows the way home. Think about it; if you knew what you
were doing, would you be here?

Sweetheart, now is the time to trust in the Lord with all
your heart. Today. He knows exactly what He's doing and
why. He has a beautiful vision for you and your life in the
future that you would not understand or believe if it were
described to you. Keep your eyes fixed straight ahead,
focused on the author of your happy ending.

12-3-12

COMING TO GRIPS WITH THE END OF YOURSELF

Those who hope in the Lord will renew their strength.
They will soar on wings like eagles;
they will run and not grow weary,
they will walk and not be faint.

ISAIAH 40:31

I am a marathon runner. Not particularly fast or talented, but one who loves the metaphor of running. I have experienced the parallels between physical and spiritual endurance, and they were a "Thomas-finger-poke" in the firmament of my faith. The doubter in me needed to touch the pain, to feel the hopelessness of my own weakness, and a marathon was God's workshop for me.

There is a place where our humanity, be it our emotional will or physical strength, simply stops. We come to the end of our personal resources. I have felt this in the midst of my divorce, and at mile 20 of a 26.2 mile marathon distance, I know what it is to come to the end of me.

Precisely then, when I am utterly spent, I call out to God, and His hand reaches for me and carries me to the end of the race. There is simply no other explanation. Isaiah 40:31 is my race day meditation. It will carry you to the finish as well.

STEPPING OUT OF DARKNESS

The moon will shine like the sun,
and the sunlight will be seven times brighter . . .
when the Lord binds up the bruises of his people.

ISAIAH 30:26

The darkness is intimidating.

I remember feeling afraid, lost, floundering, and very, very small. It was hard for me to be still long enough for my eyes to adjust, so I kept running into walls.

During this bleak time, the only thing I could find to cling to was the Lord's promise of light up ahead. Once I stood still and asked for direction, I moved shakily forward . . . step-by-step . . . into the faint hue of illumination indicative of the great light that still lies ahead of me. Darkness is not only represented in our outward circumstances, it is often found in our own internal gloom, our dismal lack of repentance, or the bleak haze of unforgiveness in our hearts.

God doesn't promise just a flashlight or even a search-light. He promises a light seven times brighter than the sun! Whatever bright memories of our old lives we cling to, let's drop them and move on into the glorious future shining in the distance.

12-8-10

THE VIEW FROM ABOVE

What is seen is temporary, but what is unseen is eternal.
2 CORINTHIANS 4:18

It seems impossible to imagine right now, from where you are, that this season is temporary. Doesn't it seem your life is defined by these circumstances? That you will feel this way forever? That this is your new reality? Wisdom speaks through God's Word. He is telling us that this pain is temporary, that we will transcend these circumstances, and that this is not the life He has in store for us.

I have often imagined myself wandering around lost in one of those huge mazes made by tall, carefully cut European shrubs. If I just sit down and cry, utterly frustrated by it all, how would I know that the path to exit is just around the next bend in the maze? I cannot see far enough in front of me to know how much farther I have to go. The mere idea of endurance without end is overwhelming to me. The only ultimate perspective is from above! God sees the beginning and the end, and every twist and turn in between.

Don't give in to weakness by dwelling on what you see today. Look through it, as hard as it is, to the vision just beyond your sight.

13·12·18

LOOKING FOR HEALING

I am the Lord, who heals you.

EXODUS 15:26

When you are hurting, many people will come out of the woodwork to present you with remedies "sure" to alleviate your pain. There are many choices in the natural world . . . yoga, therapy, acupuncture, exercise, sleeping pills, coping pills, massage, shopping too much, working too much, changes in diet, books, tapes, alcohol, sex. You name it, they will suggest it.

You may try any one or a combination of these so-called solutions. Don't beat yourself up about it if you have, because it's natural to look around for immediate relief. We have been raised in a society based on immediate gratification. If we're experiencing pain, we look for the fastest way to avoid it, and if this isn't possible, we numb it out. We have plenty of methods of avoidance and anesthesia. At some point, hopefully sooner rather than later, we come to the end of the line with these methods. We build up a tolerance to them and require more, only to grow increasingly frustrated and empty.

It is impossible to avoid pain; you must walk through it or it will wait for you around every corner. And it is impossible to numb pain; you must experience it fully to come cleanly out the other side.

The only suggestion worth heeding is the only path of true healing—Jesus Christ.

WHO HOLDS YOUR HEART?

*[The Lord] heals the brokenhearted
and binds up their wounds.*

PSALM 147:3

Gather up as many pieces of your broken heart as you can find, and take them to the altar. Place them there, at the foot of the cross. Bow and walk away. Resist the temptation to go back to collect the debris and try to place the misshapen fragments back together. Chances are, you'll miss a piece, bleed to death while you try, or attempt to force pieces that didn't fit that way to begin with.

Psalm 147 promises that the Lord will bind our wounds. Imagine Him, tenderly assessing the damage and compassionately wrapping your injuries. He experienced pain; He knows the depth of agony. He alone has the power to remedy your situation, and He promises to heal your broken heart.

I like to imagine His holy hands, radiant and glowing with the full power of creation. I picture those warm hands surrounding my heart, enclosing it completely. I like to think about how He remains in that position, guarding my heart until it is healed properly and fully. He protects me from injury until He declares me ready to love again.

12-16-12

LISTEN HERE, MISSY

Have I not commanded you? Be strong and courageous.
Do not be terrified; do not be discouraged, for the Lord
your God will be with you wherever you go.

JOSHUA 1:9

When I first heard this verse, I was a terrified woman. I was weak and wimpy and discouraged. I cried in the shower, at church, and anytime I drove alone.

These words spoke like a spear, aimed directly into my wounded heart. It was the tough love I needed from my heavenly Father. I committed this verse to memory and spoke it aloud at the first sign of fear. I took it as intended, not as a suggestion but as a command. Although I did not see myself as strong or courageous, I pretended I was—or at least that I could be because the Lord promised to be with me.

Soon enough I was no longer pretending. Something fierce and ugly would block my path, and I felt like a warrior, not a coward. So will you. It's not my promise; it's a promise from our Father.

DRESSING THE PART

Therefore put on the full armor of God, so that when the day of evil comes, you may be able to stand your ground, and after you have done everything, to stand.

EPHESIANS 6:13

Much is written in the Bible about the full armor of God—the breastplate, shield, helmet, boots, and sword. The imagery is powerful and mystical. The final sentence of Ephesians 6:13 is a statement that is majestic and stunning, profound and without frill: "and after you have done everything, to stand."

Your part is to dress properly and leave the rest to Him. You don't need to have the last word. You don't need to keep looking over your shoulder. Do what you can and then stand strong. Take God's armor: truth, righteousness, peace, faith, and salvation. Wrap yourself in these protections . . . and experience God's blessing. Then stand in strength. You can face your trials, discouragements, and challenges when you are clothed in His armor.

Stop! Be still! He will enable you to stand.

WHAT ARE YOU WAITING FOR?

The testing of your faith develops perseverance.
JAMES 1:3

Patience is more than waiting for an answer or for the
receipt of blessing.

Patience is deeper than struggling with the passage of time.

Patience is the practice of trusting even when we cannot see.

Patience forces us to focus on doing our part, while we wait
for God to do His.

Patience pinpoints areas where we must grow in order to
receive.

Patience evokes a spirit of humility because we recognize
that we are not in charge.

Patience involves seeking the Source instead of the solution.

Patience is maturity revealed.

Patience is the art of waiting, expectantly, joyfully, and quietly, when you have no idea what you are waiting for.

Patience is the ability to stand perfectly still in the vortex of
chaos, and be totally content to hang out until further
notice simply because you have no intention or desire
to move forward without His instruction.

12-18-19

RIGHT HERE, RIGHT NOW

Do not be afraid. Stand firm and you will see the deliverance the Lord will bring you today.

EXODUS 14:13

※

Want to know my favorite word from the passage above? *Today.*

I know I was delivered at Calvary, and I have assurance I will be welcomed into eternity . . . but what comfort, what power, what peace to imagine the deliverance I can receive right here, today.

Whatever you are facing today, from the molehill to the mountain, you can bring it to the Lord. He promises not only to comfort and sustain you, but also to deliver you . . .meaning He promises to carry you safely to the other side.

If you look too far ahead, beyond the immediate steps He has illuminated for you, it is easy to be overwhelmed into a state of inertia and anxiety. The future is just a series of todays, and you have been promised deliverance through each one. With that knowledge, it is powerfully possible to overcome fear.

Stand firm.

MORNIN', SUNSHINE

Weeping may remain for a night,
but rejoicing comes in the morning.

PSALM 30:5

Okay, maybe this night seems a little long . . . but hang in there, because this promise is one of my favorites.

God is telling us to hold out, to wait on Him, to weep and let it out, to steady ourselves through the dark of night and look hopefully to a new day.

The new day holds more than an absence of weeping. I remember when I thought a numb day felt good, merely in contrast to a painful one. But God promises not just relief or respite from pain—but rejoicing! Surviving isn't enough, thriving is! The Lord does not carry us through a season of trial so that we will live lives of mediocrity! Why would He bother refining us if He didn't have great plans for us? Weep tonight if you need to, but look through your circumstances and tears to the celebration dawning ahead.

Look to the joy that awaits you in the future, and the daybreak of a new phase of your life.

10-19-12

STONE CAN'T PROTECT US

I will give you a new heart and put a new
spirit in you; I will remove from you your heart
of stone and give you a heart of flesh.

EZEKIEL 36:26

After a weekend that felt like one painful test after another, I called my best friend in tears. I said, "Why won't this end? How strong does God want me to be, anyway? I can't take it anymore!"

Being a godly woman, and knowing me deeply like she does, she replied, "Perhaps it's the other way around, friend. You have been strong enough. God wants your heart to be soft and open."

I hadn't thought of it that way.

In response to heartbreak, betrayal, or shame, it is all too easy to develop a heart of stone. We think this will protect us from any more pain. Yet the problem with stone is that it feels nothing—no pain, but no love either. It is a trap that feels like self-preservation, but it is actually self-destruction.

The Lord wants to give you a heart of flesh. With His love you can emerge from a painful season of loss with a heart that is yielding, porous, and ready to receive the gifts He has waiting for you.

A Softened Heart Yields Understanding

They are darkened in their understanding and separated from the life of God because of the ignorance that is in them due to the hardening of their hearts.

EPHESIANS 4:18

The greatest upset, the greatest potential danger of this season, is not a legal concern, not a financial concern, not even ultimately the burden we carry for our children . . . but a serious matter of the heart. The only thing more painful, and with longer and more serious ramifications than a broken heart, is a frozen one.

In his letter to the Ephesians, the apostle Paul warns us of the eternal consequences of allowing our hearts to harden. He doesn't paint a pretty picture . . . ignorance, darkness, and separation from God.

A soft heart is not weak or naive. To the contrary, wisdom, experience, and faith make for a strong heart, weathered by compassion and seasoned with mercy. A hardened heart is not protected, it is merely encased in injury, and it is painfully obvious to everyone but you. You may as well go around with a T-shirt that reads "Kick me."

Ask the Lord today to give you and to guard in you a soft heart and a gentle spirit.

12-20-18

FulFILLment

...the fullness of him who fills everything in every way.
EPHESIANS 1:23

Perhaps you are becoming more aware of the empty spaces inside you . . . the longing, the ache, the nameless void that we all possess. We live in a frenzy to avoid this ache or in a desperate attempt to fill the space with anything we can get our hands on. We pile things into this internal cavern, not realizing that everything is falling through holes below. Being busy, or distracted, or pretending . . . none of these methods bring any relief.

Pain can be a great clarifier. If you choose, you can own up to the empty spaces. Admit to their existence and to the fact that they are causing you to bleed spiritually. Jesus is the living water. He can pour into your spirit and take up all the empty space within you. No opening is too small for water, even the smallest crack. No cistern is too large, for He is the limitless wellspring of life.

Ask Him to pour His cool, refreshing spiritual water into you. He will cleanse the dust, soothe the ache, and fill the emptiness with the fullness of *Him who fills everything in every way.*

The Willingness to Emerge

He is a child without wisdom; when the time arrives,
he does not come to the opening of the womb.

HOSEA 13:13

As Christians we have two births, a natural birth and a spiritual birth. One is of the flesh and the next is a birth of faith.

This awakening comes to different people at different times, depending on readiness, maturity, openness, and levels of pride and self-sufficiency. Some people are so pure of faith that this spiritual birth happens in childhood. Others, like me, have to work to get there with a combination of effort and the circumstantial stripping down of layers of independence.

Regardless of how we get to the spiritual labor/delivery room at our appointed time—unlike a natural birth, this time we must be willing to be reborn. We cannot remain in darkness and isolation when the time comes for us to be pushed into the world as a new creation.

YOU SEEM DIFFERENT SOMEHOW

See, I am doing a new thing! Now it springs up;
do you not perceive it?

ISAIAH 43:19

Nature is full of examples of radical change. A snake slithering out of old dull skin, revealing brilliant and defined coloration and shine. A butterfly emerging from time cloistered within the cocoon. The metamorphosis of the tadpole.

We know God created man above all creatures, to reflect His likeness and glory. So we too can expect to experience transformation of equally grand proportion.

Have you allowed others to box you in with their perspectives? Have you followed suit by diminishing your potential with self-imposed limitations? By asking God to define us, and believing only what He says about us, we can make great strides in becoming the godly women we were created to be. Even if you don't feel new yet, you can start doing things in a new way. Change begins in the heart, moves to the mind, and is expressed through action.

It's time to do a new thing. Ask the Lord to provide you a greater vision of yourself. Soon enough, people will perceive the new you.

DAY 21

You d...
bi...

FAMOUS

The gra...

1-5-13

Our vision now is ... a canvas, lyrics with... saw puzzle, an unfinis... side of needlepoint. W... what is unexplained. It ... per- spective because we are th... ...Master.

In my small and untr... ...ay, I am an artist. I craft words, and I like to paint. If someone were to walk into my studio, they would see me in my paint-spattered work shirt with dirty fingernails, the mess of mixed oils on my palette, sticky brushes, stained carpet beneath my easel, and inexplicable color forms on canvas—and most likely would be highly unimpressed. The process of creation can be messy.

The Creator of the universe alone knows the final outcome of the artistry of our lives. We may not understand His methods or fully appreciate His technique, but we can trust that He knows His craft.

We have to trust, even in the face of great confusion, chaos, or peril, that He has great beauty in mind for us.

e of our Lord was poured out
on me abundantly.

1 TIMOTHY 1:14

Take great comfort in these words of truth.

If you are an impatient woman—one who flips to the last chapter or wants to hear about movies you haven't seen, or searched for hidden Christmas presents as a child, take heart, because this Scripture is your happy ending.

When you flip to your life's last page, these words complete your story. Regardless of all the trials you endure and the twists and turns of your path, this is the outcome of your story.

As an old woman you will reflect over the days of your life and conclude that "the grace of our Lord was poured out on me abundantly."

1-5-13

TELL ME, FATHER

Ask the Lord your God for a sign.

ISAIAH 7:11

Do you ever go off on your own, making your own plans and creating your own scenarios, only to realize when the first glitch or roadblock presents itself that you have neglected to run your idea by God first? I am really working on this one! I need to ask God for direction first, instead of choosing my course and then asking Him to bless my mess.

The Lord is not only a "Sunday God." He wants to be our premier confidant all week long. He wants to be involved in the daily happenings of life. He longs to be the first person we call on, the first person we cry with or celebrate with, the first opinion we seek.

If you are looking to make any changes in your life, work on consulting God first. Ask Him for a sign.

1-6-13

NO DEAD END

With my God I can scale a wall.

PSALM 18:29

I like a good, scary movie.

Often there is a chase scene where someone is being pursued at night through a bad part of town. Inevitably they take a wrong turn down an alley and end up at a dead end. The fear and futility of scenes like this leave me breathless.

Perhaps it resonates with me because I have been chased down by the enemy in a similar symbolic fashion. I have taken my share of wrong turns. But with the Lord, there are no dead ends! We see things in only one perspective, our own. God sees many levels. He knows when we have come to the end of our ability and He provides an alternate route. Many of the walls that hem us in are of our own construction.

By my God I can leap over a wall.

Commit this verse to memory, and the next time you feel cornered, jump!

No Small Responsibility

*And he has committed to us the message of
reconciliation. We are therefore Christ's ambassadors,
as though God were making his appeal through us.*

2 CORINTHIANS 5:19-20

As much as you may not like it, people are watching you
right now.

Just like a highway accident causes traffic delays in the
opposite direction, the world is also filled with emotional
"rubberneckers" . . . people who slow to watch other people's
lives. Perhaps part of it is curiosity, part is bad manners,
another part is fear. "What if this happened to me?" "What
would I do?" "I wonder what she did to deserve this?"

People are watching to see how you handle this . . .
what you do, how you act, the choices you make. They are
talking about you behind your back, placing bets on how
you will fare. I don't say this to upset you; I say this to illustrate the scope of the opportunity at hand. Use this
unwanted attention to be a light for Christ. Heal properly.
Continue to love. Make godly, wise decisions. Take the high
road. Take your time.

Then, later, when someone asks you, "How on earth
did you do it?" you will be prepared to respond with
enlightenment—giving credit where credit is due.

1-9-13

A Purer Heart

The crucible for silver and the furnace for gold,
but the Lord tests the heart.

PROVERBS 17:3

The crucible crushes impurities, and the furnace burns them away. I have witnessed similar circumstances in my life—sustaining massive wounds to my heart as areas of my life were stripped away. I don't know why it has to hurt so much; perhaps later it will all make sense when I have the proper eyes to grant perspective.

One night my son Luke awoke, crying in pain with leg cramps or "growing pains." I held him and massaged his legs, explaining to him how his bones and muscles were getting so big and strong.

He said, "Why does it have to hurt to grow, Mommy?"

At that moment, I felt a bolt of understanding into my own circumstances. It just plain hurts to grow. Certain things (dreams, people, eras) are left behind, and our journey continues. We are spiritually pared down, exchanging things and people for weightless treasures like wisdom and understanding.

The Lord is testing your heart. As much as it hurts, let Him have His way with you.

A FIERY TRIAL

They saw that the fire had not harmed their bodies, nor was a hair of their heads singed; their robes were not scorched, and there was no smell of fire on them.

DANIEL 3:27

୨ଛ

The king threw Shadrach, Meshach, and Abednego into the fire because they would not worship his gods. Their loyalty to God cost them a trip to the furnace, but they were not dismayed. Rather than fearfully recant their faith, they spoke their truth and faced the repercussions. What became of them in the fire? Nothing! They were utterly unharmed.

God rewards us with His protection and provision when we remain true to Him. Sometimes we are delivered unscathed; other times we are purified in the heat. Whatever the worldly consequences may be, we will never walk through them without His company. We will never face trials without His knowledge.

The king saw four figures in the fire that day, although there were three men thrown in. The Lord promises never to leave or forsake us in our hour of need.

For no other god can save in this way (v. 29).

CLOSE TO THE FLAME

I will surely save you out of a distant place...
I will not completely destroy you. I will
discipline you but only with justice.

JEREMIAH 30:10-11

During my own season of discipline and penance, I flinched several times as the Lord brought me closer to the purifying flame. He intimately knows all our thresholds and does not take us beyond what we can bear.

Wounded, I felt sorry for myself, but someone graciously pointed out to me that if God had no special plans for me or no interest in refining and strengthening me, He would never go to these lengths. It gave me courage and endurance to know He felt I was worthy of His attention. I felt significant because He was apparently supervising my growth. It made me want to please Him by responding well to His spiritual boot camp.

I figured as long as it was going to hurt anyway, as long as I was committed to doing the work, I may as well go as deep as possible. He kept His word and saved me out of this distant place.

1-15-13

A TEMPEST'S TREASURE

Look, he is coming with the clouds.
REVELATION 1:7

1-15-17

Clouds. Times of tempests and confusion, darkness and doubt, weakness and fear. When our usual warmth, ease, and clear vision of the sun is obscured, this is when the Lord arrives. Take heart when the thunder crashes and you think the next bolt of lightning is aimed at you. Contrary to our very human nature, when the clouds roll in and everything appears bleak, the greatest clearing is about to enter our personal skyline.

Noah didn't exactly have good weather. Neither did the disciples when they were tossed about in the boat while Jesus slept peacefully below deck. We were never told to expect clear skies and plenty of sun. For generations we have been taught to expect the storms of life, and not only that, but to be of good cheer. Why? Because Jesus has already overcome the world. He waits until the moment is right, and the storm swirls and rages in our lives. He waits for us to scan the skies, looking for His presence in the clouds. He wants us to sleep peacefully throughout, knowing that at the gesture of His hand, He can quiet wind and waves.

Don't be afraid of clouds.

CLEAN UP YOUR ACT

*Get rid of all bitterness, rage and anger, brawling
and slander, along with every form of malice.
Be kind and compassionate to one another, forgiving
each other, just as in Christ God forgave you.*

EPHESIANS 4:31–32

Gulp.

Yes, this one is a biggie. I kept this verse on the windowsill by my kitchen sink for many, many months. When God was telling me to get rid of these poisonous things, it seemed daunting. Over time He directed me to work on some things, other things to simply let go. The very idea of generating feelings of kindness for someone who has broken your heart seems at the very least ridiculous, and at the most . . . impossible.

The trick is that it is not at all about feelings. He doesn't say, "Feel kind and compassionate toward one another." He says, "Be kind and compassionate to one another." It's an order, requiring simple obedience, not emotion. Obedience springs from the love and desire to please God, nothing else.

We are called to forgive because we have been forgiven, and to love because we have been loved.

STRENGTH FOR CLIMBING

You have stayed long enough at this mountain.
DEUTERONOMY 1:6

A year of trials includes many mountains to scale:

The mountain of despair.

The mountain of regret.

The mountain of anger.

The mountain of bitterness.

The mountain of unforgiveness.

The mountain of sadness.

The mountain of doubt.

The mountain of loneliness.

The mountain of change.

These mountains take time. You may sit awhile in the intimidating shadow in the valley of a mountain. You may have several false starts in choosing the best path of ascension. You may fall flat on your face, skidding uncontrollably down the other side. Each climb is grueling and exhausting. Listen to the voice of God as your Sherpa. He will carry your heavy load. He will provide safe footing on the path. He will be your safety rope as you rappel down the rock face.

He will be your holy timekeeper, telling you, His precious daughter, "Enough is enough. It's time to move on."

1-18-13

MOUNTAIN-SIZED FAITH

I tell you the truth, if anyone says to this mountain,
"Go, throw yourself into the sea," and does not doubt
in his heart but believes that what he says will
happen, it will be done for him.

MARK 11:23

Oh, how I long for faith like this!

I want to be a woman without doubt.

We all have mountains in our lives. Mountains are the things that seem insurmountable—too grand to scale, too deep to burrow beneath, and too massive to go around. We may spend so long fretting at the foot of our mountain that we set up a base camp and prepare to live this way, in the shadow of our own fear. I pray to God to become a woman of such power in faith that I can boldly command the mountains in my life to, "Go, throw yourself into the sea."

And then, in an act of bold expectation, I can turn my face to avoid the spray of the ocean splash. I can continue right on my way, walking barefoot through the soft, freshly turned earth where my mountain used to be.

CHILDLIKE FAITH FOR GROWN-UP DREAMS

*Therefore, if anyone is in Christ, he is a new creation;
the old has gone, the new has come!*
2 CORINTHIANS 5:17

Do you remember being a little girl, playing dress-up and twirling in front of a mirror? Do you remember how beautiful you felt? Do you recall what you dreamed of when you were a child? Perhaps you envisioned a significant career, your own family, a deep faith, rich friendships, and a lifelong marriage.

Sadly, life doesn't always turn out as we plan. Those sweet dreams of our youth are often replaced by the harsh realities of life. Remember that God never asks us to settle for anything less than what He intends; we are the ones who settle. We are the ones who play small to make ourselves more pleasing to those with a limited view.

Change hurts, I know it does. But it is also a time to reflect and remember how you used to see yourself. You can undergo a spiritual makeover and be a new creation in Christ. Resurrect your youthful dreams and the fairy tale that you dismissed as impossible. Nothing is impossible with God.

1-18-13

FRAME IT GOD'S WAY

The wise woman builds her house.

PROVERBS 14:1

Right now it probably seems like the careful construction of your home and your family is in rubble all around you. On some of my darker days, I felt like a woman after a house fire, sifting through burned treasures in the ashes.

But sometimes it takes a pile of rubble to prepare the way for a major remodel.

Yes, life as you knew it is no longer. However, there is an inherent gift in the debris. You can prayerfully, purposefully, patiently be the architect and builder of your new home. Let Scripture and prayer be your blueprint; choose your materials wisely.

Did your children have an ungodly environment before? Start praying together. Did you walk on eggshells? Start dancing in stilettos. Did tension hum? Start singing. Do it differently. Do it better. Do it God's way. Make it your way.

1-23-13

WHAT DOES FREEDOM LOOK LIKE TO YOU?

It is for freedom that Christ has set us free.
Stand firm, then, and do not let yourselves
be burdened again by a yoke of slavery.
GALATIANS 5:1

Jesus died on the cross for our redemption, ultimately, our freedom. He did not set us free so we could be miserable. He did not set us free so we could be depressed. He did not set us free so we could be prisoners to regret. He did not set us free so we could live in a fiery cloud of anger and bitterness. He did not set us free so we could be numb. He did not set us free to go through the motions and call that life.

He set us free for freedom. Read that again, will you? If you don't feel excited by that idea, read it yet again.

Free! What does that mean to you? I see a woman laughing, her hair blowing while riding in a convertible. A toddler exploring on chubby, uncertain legs. A dolphin leaping, chasing waves. A retirement party and an awaiting sailboat. A rope swing over water. Tan, bare feet on the beach.

We don't need to remain yoked to our old lives, our old selves. Let's pray for one another, for the strength to stand firm in our freedom.

REACHING THE SPRING

*Now to him who is able to do immeasurably more
than all we ask or imagine, according to his
power that is at work within us.*

EPHESIANS 3:20

When times are tough, the cliché is that you have to dig deep. Just like digging a well, you go deeper and deeper until you hit water. When we search deep within, we run into the wellspring of life . . . the very core of us, beyond the body, beyond the mind, beyond emotion, where the soul resides. When we dig deep enough to hit that spring, we know we have found sustenance forever. That is the place Paul refers to; the place where the power is at work within us.

True change commences from this place. The quiet stirring becomes a wave that radiates to all the numb and deprived areas of our existence and beyond, out to others.

How miraculous to know that as a reward for digging deep enough to reach Him, He is able to do immeasurably more than all we ask or imagine.

Read that statement again, because no matter how you try, you cannot place a limit on it.

SETTLE DOWN

Be still, and know that I am God.

PSALM 46:10

We women, in our innate desire to be all things to all people, are frantic. We rush around in a blur of car pools, meetings, exercise, and the frantic hustle of what it takes to make households, careers, and relationships run. We take on more than our share and quietly resent the fact that our inner reserve has long ago gone dry.

We need to tie a tourniquet on this wound of busyness. If we don't, we will soon bleed a spiritual death. Doing more and doing it faster is not taking us to a place of peace. The distraction it provides is nothing more than a momentary escape. Sooner or later we have to stop to take a breath. Often when we are forced to be still, the magnitude of the weight we carry becomes enormous, the loneliness unbearable. We think momentum keeps us from thinking . . . from feeling . . . from knowing . . . from going there.

Where do you go to get alone with God? Do you even know? Find out. Go there, alone, and be still. Sit long enough for the awareness to overcome you; that your burden is not meant for you to shoulder alone.

FIRST THINGS FIRST

*But seek first his kingdom and his righteousness,
and all these things will be given to you as well.*

MATTHEW 6:33

We always have time for the thing we put first.

I set my alarm so I can pray before the rush of the day overtakes me. If I miss that prayer window, I pray while I drive or run. No matter how busy or crazy my day becomes, I am always out in front of Luke's elementary school at 2:45 p.m. I find time to return important phone calls. Most days I manage to find time to exercise. I find time, or make time, to write; usually in a scribbled notebook at doctors' offices, in carpool lines, or while watching soccer practice.

From these statements it is safe to say I value my faith, my children, my family, my friends, my fitness, and my career.

Sometimes I feel centered and steady, other times a scattered mess. When I am overwhelmed, the root of the lack of equilibrium can always be traced back to one thing—my time (or lack of it) spent with God.

If I have managed to let other things or people slip ahead of Him on my priority list, I can feel the effects in all areas of my life in no time flat.

When I seek Him first, daily, decision by decision, all other things can pile on and my peace, balance, and confidence are never disturbed.

CRY TO THE LORD

*To the Lord I cry aloud, and he answers
me from his holy hill.*

PSALM 3:4

A godly girlfriend of mine has a saying, "Go to the throne,
not the phone." She's right. No girlfriend or therapist can
be there in every moment of need, pain, or desperation. No
human being can or should be put in the position to carry
our load of grief. Cry to the Lord. Go ahead. Yell, rant,
vent, cry . . . all of it. He can take it. In fact, He wants to
take it. His Word tells us that He longs to exchange burdens
with us; so let Him carry your junk for a while. Tell Him
how angry you are. Explain to Him all the ways you have
been hurt and betrayed. The Lord knows everything about
pain and betrayal—after all, He was handed over to an ago-
nizing death on the cross by the kiss of a friend.

All human beings are imperfect. Every person will fail
you to some degree, at some point. Choose a heavenly confidant. The Lord will endure all your grief, wipe all your
tears, keep safe all your secrets, and whisper words that truly
have the power to heal.

1-26-13

HE ALREADY KNOWS

Before they call I will answer;
while they are still speaking I will hear.

ISAIAH 65:24

God knows the desires of our hearts without our uttering a word.

I can take one look at my child, or hear the tone of voice, and tell you if they are tired, hurting, silly, or sad . . . and I am a mediocre parent compared to our heavenly Father.

So you might say if He already knows what I need or what is wrong, why pray?

Because prayer is a time of relationship, not request.

It's a time to seek not merely an answer, but the presence of the One who knows. It's a time to rest in the company of our Maker and know that He is God. He wants us to come to Him, to call on Him; He longs to hear our voices and offer kindness to His children. When someone you love chooses you first when they need help or comfort, it is an honor. God feels the same way.

When someone loves you, do you tire of hearing it?

Neither does He.

TRUSTING GOD TO PROVIDE

Test me in this . . . and see if I will not throw open the floodgates of heaven and pour out so much blessing that you will not have room enough for it.

MALACHI 3:10

Are you *kidding* me?

The floodgates of heaven, bursting open for me?

Blessings I cannot contain? Overflowing?

This is not some lucky cookie at a Chinese restaurant, honey; this is the Word of God! This is a timeless promise of not just provision but of bounty. You may be tempted to worry about your finances and the future stability of your household in monetary terms. You may be tempted by fear to cling or withhold when God is asking you to give. We must abide in the truth that the Lord will provide for us. The Lord asks us to test Him here on His Word.

How do we do that? We test this promise by being obedient, by trusting Him equally in times of joy and despair, and by building a spirit of patience . . . knowing that He alone knows how, and when, and why.

THE WORTHY QUESTION

You do not have, because you do not ask God.

JAMES 4:2

You mean I can have whatever I want?

No. (Sorry.)

This Scripture is one that I have to really pray over to gain insight because it is deceptively simple. I have struggled toward the conclusion that the meaning has something to do with learning how to ask the right questions.

For effective prayer, our hearts must be rightly related to God. We must be clear of resentment, unforgiveness, and areas of pride and selfishness. To be truly repentant and humble, we cannot cling even to confessed sin. From this place, we can think about approaching the throne of grace. We must grow in faith to learn to ask for things in accordance with God's will, not our own.

I have come to this place before, the throne room, and when I do, my petty list of requests and petitions falls from my hands. I drop to my knees and manage only, "Can You show me what to ask for?"

Maybe this is the only question worth asking.

RECOGNIZING YOUR NEED

"What do you want me to do for you?" [Jesus] asked.
MARK 10:36

Do you know your own heart well enough that if the Savior of the world asked you this question, your answer would be ready?

Of course He knows our needs and desires before we can even collect our thoughts to form intelligible sentences of prayer.

But He loves to hear us ask. He loves how we rely on Him. He loves how we trust Him to fill our empty places. We experience more growth by learning to ask our questions than we do by receiving answers. If we ask Him, He will draw us closer to Him, and in doing so, we will have a clearer vision of ourselves. Learning to recognize our needs returns us full circle, back again to our Father.

He asks us kindly, like a loving father to His precious little girl, "What do you want me to do for you?"

Heal me.

Renew me.

Restore me.

Elevate me.

Bless me.

Teach me.

Love me.

OPEN TO LOVE

There is no fear in love. But perfect love drives out fear.

1 JOHN 4:18

The prospect of building a new life and embracing new love is intimidating—especially after a failed marriage. If we reflect too deeply on mistakes of the past, we are mired in the shadows between old and new. Our God is intimately relational, and women in particular are made in this aspect of His likeness.

We too are relational to the center of our being. We are not meant to be alone. We are not created to fear love.

Openness to new experiences of love through many avenues in our lives (children, ministry, beauty in nature, friendships, new romantic love) is something worthy to pray for. We don't have to fear a broken heart (we have experienced that and lived!) because we know that the Lord is guarding our hearts, shielding us from the burden of this responsibility.

Perfect love casts out fear. No love on earth is perfect—that is certain. But God's love is perfect. And He wants us to be free to love, which sometimes entails loss, without fear.

2-4-13

FREEDOM FROM FEAR

For God did not give us a spirit of timidity,
but a spirit of power, of love and of self-discipline.
2 TIMOTHY 1:7

What are you afraid of?

I am afraid of failure, rejection, intense pain, and speaking my deepest truths.

Fear traps us. It takes away our power and reduces our influence. Timidity and trepidation keep us tethered where God wants us to fly.

In Paul's statement to Timothy, notice he does not say that God refers to those "strong, courageous, powerful, and influential other people who do amazing things." No, he says simply "us." He means you and me.

The Lord wants us to look our fear straight in the eyes and see it clearly. I am afraid of failure and rejection and managed to survive divorce. Not only that, I must try to truly love again. I am wary of intense pain yet gave birth to three children and I run marathons. I fear speaking my deepest truths, yet you are holding this book.

By showing us our fear through our scars, God bears witness to His healing strength in spite of ourselves.

Again, I ask you, what are you afraid of?

2-12-13

REFUGE FROM FEAR

Come near to God and he will come near to you.

JAMES 4:8

❧

Fear is a dangerous thing.

It can paralyze us. It can also propel us.

Learn to recognize fear and your reaction to it, because this knowledge of yourself will equip you to be prepared. Do you freeze into submission or inertia? Or do you burst forth foolishly in any direction, just to get away or keep moving?

Once you have learned this about yourself, you can begin to recognize what frightens you and how to handle it. The demise of a relationship, the breakdown of a family, the loss of a dream, the prospect of facing life alone . . . these are scary things by anyone's standards. Don't shy from them, name them! Call them by what they are and take away their power over your life. Go to God . . . not as a last resort but at the first twinge of uncertainty or nervousness. Take a step in the right direction, and He will always meet you there.

SACRED PLACES

God is our refuge and strength,
an ever-present help in trouble.
PSALM 46:1

Outside my kitchen I have a screened-in porch that I dearly love. It's where I often feed my kids, where we do art projects, where I drink my coffee in the morning and sometimes enjoy a glass of wine late at night. It's my favorite spot to read, pray, and write.

Texas has some awesome rainstorms—big, booming, and sudden. When the sky begins to blacken and the wind picks up, the kids and I head for the porch. It is an incredible feeling to be dry and safe while a storm rages all around you.

This is the internal sanctuary we have in the Lord. When storms rage around us, we have a place of refuge that is cozy and secure. The more we know Jesus, the more swiftly we can access this shelter.

Throughout the day, practice the route to peace. That way, when you feel a storm brewing, you will move automatically to a place of protection.

BREATHE

*From the Lord comes deliverance. May your
blessing be on your people. Selah*

PSALM 3:8

I love to linger over the book of Psalms before I go to bed. I find the psalms hopeful and comforting and they make for a restful night's sleep. I used to see the word *Selah* in my reading and skip over it because I had no idea what it meant.

Just recently I learned that *Selah* means "pause" . . . literally, stop, rest, and reflect.

As a single mother of three young children, I know I don't make enough time in my life for *Selah*. We can't expect God to talk to us when we don't slow down long enough to center ourselves in His presence and wait for His voice. We place greater emphasis on *doing* than we do on *being*. We ignore the importance of rest. We are afraid to reflect, because it might involve seeing things we prefer not to see.

Things like deliverance and blessing are no quick fix—these good things take time. With time comes patience. With patience comes understanding. And with understanding comes wisdom. And with wisdom comes freedom.

Selah.

FRESH GRACE

Because of the Lord's great love we are not consumed,
for his compassions never fail. They are new
every morning; great is your faithfulness.
LAMENTATIONS 3:22–23

My home is noisy and chaotic, exploding with the energy of three small children. Each school day is a race against the clock to get kids up, dressed, and out the door with shoes, lunches, and backpacks. I am breathless and exhausted by 9:00 a.m.

But I am not depleted.

I have learned what I need to do to stay centered. My children need to be up at 6:45 so I set my alarm for 6:00. I enjoy the solitude of a sleeping house while I grab a cup of coffee and plop on the sofa with my Bible and a couple of my favorite devotionals. I read Scripture the way I used to read horoscopes, knowing that there is a message encrypted just for me. I find the nourishment I need for that day, and take God up on His daily offer of fresh compassion in the morning.

I believe there is a reason He tells us to seek Him in the morning. My day is totally off when I miss my quiet time. Things that normally do not faze me when I have started my day with the Lord send me into a tailspin when I am spiritually empty. When I begin my day in His company I am equipped to handle whatever the day brings, knowing every moment is planned for, and I am not alone.

A Command for Life

Live in peace with each other.
1 THESSALONIANS 5:13

Living in peace with each other does not mean we agree with each other, desire each other's company or feel warmly toward one another.

Peace is not just the absence of malice, but the presence of love.

We think too often of love in terms of romance, passion, or marriage. Agape love is the love God calls us to, and it is a higher, all-encompassing love. It is not related to emotion or based in things as fleeting as passion or present circumstances. It is based solely in God.

We are called to live in peace. It is a mandate, not a suggestion. Jesus lived in peace every moment of His life, even to His death, and we are called to emulate Him. We don't have to desire this, understand how to do this, or conjure the feelings associated with it. We simply have to obey, ask for help, and open ourselves to the power of agape love.

HOLINESS IS IN THE DETAILS

If they continue in faith, love and holiness . . .
1 TIMOTHY 2:15

A clean car, fresh flowers, a candle burning, the smell of laundry drying or something baking, clean sheets on my bed, a soak in my tub . . . regardless of what else is happening out in the world, these are the small details that speak peace to my soul.

It is important to guard our details and be mindful of what gives us rest. We need to know the little things that grant refuge within chaos. We may not know it, but God is in these small details. These are His messages that everything is going to be okay.

God does not want us to become tainted by our circumstances. He wants us to remain intact in spite of them. The love and faithfulness that reside within us are of God.

They are not imparted by another person.

They cannot be impacted by another person.

This means they can never leave us. Nor can anyone take them from us. Love and faithfulness are part of us, woven into the fibers of God's children. They are God's essence imparted to us.

A Jewel in the Debris

All your sons shall be taught by the Lord,
and great will be your children's peace.

ISAIAH 54:13

The greatest gift of my divorce was in allowing me to create a faith-filled home in which to raise my children. As mothers, we all worry about how everything impacts the hearts and minds of our children. The magnitude of divorce in this sense is utterly overwhelming.

Yet, I have gleaned a priceless jewel in the debris. For better or worse my children look to me. They look to me to see how merciful and generous I am in good times. They look to me to see how strong and faithful I am in bad times. They watch, they listen, and they model. Years from now I want my children to remember a childhood lived well, with a mother who was loving, consistent, devoted, funny, disciplined, playful, and totally present and emotionally available.

I carry the weight of that responsibility like a small, smooth stone in my pocket. Always there, always a reminder of how my choices affect others . . . how my healing matters greatly, how love ultimately always prevails, and how the indisputable essence of forgiveness frees us all.

May the peace of our children be great.

YES, YOU ARE

The King is enthralled by your beauty.
PSALM 45:11

Who, me?

Puffy eyes? Dark circles? Too skinny? Overweight? A few years and a few children under my belt?

Beautiful?

Yes, you. Me. All women everywhere. We all are lovely in the eyes of God. Always. He created us and loves us just as we are, the princesses He intended from the time we were little girls. We are the pinnacle, His finishing touch on creation. We represent the comfort of beauty, a brilliant facet of our God.

If you aren't feeling particularly beautiful, ask God to help you reconnect with your beauty on the inside. Ask Him to help you find your peace, which radiates out to others as nothing less than pure magnetism . . . alluring others to come to God, if for no other reason than to discover what it is that makes you shine.

Smile and be at rest; the King is indeed enthralled by your beauty.

A SPIRITUAL MAKEOVER

He who was seated on the throne said,
"I am making everything new!"
REVELATION 21:5

Look at any women's magazine and it's easy to find articles about makeovers. What is it about us that makes us want to pore over "before" and "after" photos? Perhaps because we were created to love beauty and we are hopeful to the very core. No matter how badly we have let things go, we still have little-girl dreams of redemption and transformation.

Does your life feel like a "before" picture? It's okay to admit that, because God is interested in more than your surface beauty. He wants to make over your whole life! He wants to change the way you think, which impacts how you feel, which translates into the actions and choices that build a life of good character.

He wants to help you build a new life, one that reflects His glory and His plan for you.

A CHANGE OF HEART

Give me your heart and let your eyes keep to my ways.
PROVERBS 23:26

How do you see yourself? As someone downtrodden and depressed? Someone not worthy of being cherished? Someone without hope for a second chance? Someone who can't make it on her own? Someone who deserves to be betrayed or abandoned?

Newsflash—this is not how God views you as His precious daughter! He loves you, cherishes you, is faithful to you, is honest with you, and will never leave you. The way you see yourself determines the depth and amount of God's favor you will *be able to receive* (not how much He will *give* you, which is limitless). Craft a list of all the traits you admire and prepare to grasp the idea that these traits are meant to describe you.

He longs to renew your mind to better align your thinking with His thinking; the nature of your heart with the nature of His.

Allow Him access to your thoughts. Become the woman He thinks of you as in His heart.

BEAUTY IS LIGHT

*Your beauty should not come from outward
adornment . . . Instead, it should be that of your inner
self, the unfading beauty of a gentle and quiet spirit,
which is of great worth in God's sight.*

1 PETER 3:3–4

If you have been hurt or betrayed, or if you have hurt or
betrayed someone, chances are you do not feel very beautiful.

Beauty does not derive from outward adornment, like
clothes, makeup, jewelry, and other ways we present ourselves
to the world. Nor does it come from outward sources like
feelings or present circumstances. It is not exclusive, meant
only for those on the covers of magazines. It is the essence of
anyone who invites the Holy Spirit to dwell within.

Beauty is a reflection of God's light refracted through
your presence.

Beauty, like love, cannot be pursued or forced. It has to
be inhabited.

It is a refining process of becoming your full and glorious self in Christ. Quit striving, it doesn't make you more
beautiful, and it won't cover your pain. You fool no one.

Instead, cultivate a gentle and quiet spirit of rest, and
relax into being yourself.

CELEBRATE THE WOMAN YOU ARE

We have different gifts, according to the grace given us.
ROMANS 12:6

It is such a sorrowful waste of energy and spirit to grieve the woman you are not. Based on worldly standards, there will always be someone smarter, funnier, younger, thinner, wealthier, or prettier than you.

Reread that, soak it in, and then promptly get over it.

Step one to your recovery is to get over yourself. And when you have done that, you can begin to be useful to God.

Instead of grieving the woman you are not, ask the Lord to show you how to celebrate the woman you are. He will reveal your gifts to you slowly, in direct proportion to your readiness to understand, use, and appreciate them. And when He shows you your gifts, you will want nothing more than to use them to glorify the Giver.

Will you get over yourself today?

DEEP ROOTS YIELD LUSH FOLIAGE

*They will be called oaks of righteousness, a planting of
the Lord for the display of his splendor.*

ISAIAH 61:3

God didn't create women to be wilted or weak. Our gender
has a bizarre tendency to minimize our needs and to belittle our own glory. Why do we play down? To make ourselves less threatening? To whom? Why do we equate this
minimization with accessibility? We are not making others
more comfortable by playing small. In fact, we are sending
the message to others that they need to play down, too. I
am not encouraging pridefulness but to be authentic by
sharing the gift of our true selves.

Our strength is desperately desired. Our beauty is sorely absent when we stifle it. Our unique offerings are missed
when we hide.

We were created by the Lord to display His splendor!

Root yourself as a creation in Christ. Align yourself to
assure the nutrients and sunshine you require to grow into
the majestic, powerful beauty God intended.

Eyes of Faith

He touched their eyes and said,
"According to your faith will it be done to you."
MATTHEW 9:29

We are defined by the way we see ourselves.

Do you see a healthy, confident woman, whole and healed, worthy of lasting love and the eternal blessing of God's favor?

Do you see yourself moving joyfully, freely, and successfully along God's chosen path for you?

Do you see health and abundance for you and your family?

Do you see a vision of your life story bringing pleasure to your Creator?

Do you see yourself expanded by grace and gratitude?

If your view of yourself is puny, ask the Lord to touch your eyes. Step out in faith and request a new vision. Begin to sense the divine in your own possibility. Create a vision that makes your heart overflow with excitement and wonder. Once you see with eyes of faith and create the space, God will step in and fill it.

Remember, according to your faith will it be done to you.

THAT KIND OF WOMAN

You know that the testing of your faith develops persever-
ance. Perseverance must finish its work so that you may
be mature and complete, not lacking anything.

JAMES 1:3–4

Have you had the incredible good fortune to spend time in the company of a spiritually mature woman? Her presence, emanating from her gracious and fully open heart, simultaneously soothes and inspires. People of both sexes long to be near her. She is warm, intuitive, and radiates the peace of a person comfortable in her own skin.

Her level of comfort with herself is disarming, allowing everyone around her to relax and be fully themselves, fully present in the moment. She is not constantly reaching, doing, or wielding her power. She doesn't need to. She is awesomely at rest in the embodiment of herself.

My grandmother Millie G. is this kind of woman. When I spend time with her, I see the way I want to age, the direction I want to grow, the way I want to blossom spiritually, and the way I want to nurture those around me.

She is complete in Christ. She lacks nothing. Her contentment is contagious, her peace palpable, and her influence divine.

YOUR JOB NOW

He who wins souls is wise.

PROVERBS 11:30

❧

There is no point to suffering if no redeeming good results from it. You are not being tested merely to receive a grade on your report card. You are being honed to become a blessing and an encouragement to others. You are being instructed in the fine art of winning souls.

Does the very idea of evangelism seem foreign to you? Do you say, "Oh, that's not my personality or my spiritual gift"? Evangelism is not limited to those with signs on street corners, those with eloquence behind the pulpit, those who reach thousands over satellite TV, or those who ring doorbells and hand out Bibles.

Evangelism can be as subtle and as powerful as a teary friend asking you, "How do you do it? You seem so 'okay.'" And you take a deep breath, and you tell her the Truth.

Prepare to Be Used

Be wise in the way you act toward outsiders; make the most of every opportunity.

COLOSSIANS 4:5

You can be certain after you have walked through any difficult season in life that the Lord intends to use you. He has been using the heat of your trial to mold and perfect you. He has softened your heart so that you will be the embrace of mercy and the voice of compassion and wisdom to others in the future.

Soon enough, this will become clear to you as you see numerous circumstances as being more than coincidental. These are divine appointments, for which you will need to be open and ready. Your humility and compassion will invite others who are similarly suffering to be drawn to you. You will be the hands and feet of Jesus, ministering to His beloved.

This has been the training ground, and you have been here for a reason. Remember, He works all things together for good. He wouldn't have pruned you so carefully if He did not plan for you to bear fruit.

Open yourself to make the most of every opportunity.

TIES THAT BIND

Where you go I will go, and where you stay I will stay.
Your people will be my people and your God my God.

RUTH 1:16

Although this Scripture is part of many weddings, it was actually a conversation between two women—Ruth and Naomi. It illustrates the fierce devotion, loyalty, and deep love between female friends. Ruth lost her husband and chose to follow her mother-in-law, Naomi, instead of returning home to her own people. Sometimes love between friends can heal us in ways our families of origin cannot. God defines family in many ways. We have our original family, our extended family, our family of friends, our family in Christ. Blood makes a family, but so does love.

Remember slumber parties, playing with one another's hair and talking and laughing deep into the night? That bliss of friendship is not reserved only for young girls. It is available and desirable to all of us, at any age. God knew we needed each other. He intended us to live in community and share our lives with one another.

Think of the girlfriends you cherish today. Thank God for them. Call them. Write to them. See them. Love them. Pray with them. Care for them. Appreciate them.

God loves loving you through your friends.

A Priceless Gift

*My intercessor is my friend as my eyes
pour out tears to God.*

JOB 16:20

A real friend is God's evidence on earth of His love for you.

A real friend is a channel between you and God, a conduit for the Holy Spirit. Her words are the Lord's wisdom, spoken to you in a voice as familiar and warm as your favorite robe.

A real friend does not judge; she invites you to examine. A real friend does not direct; she invites you to pray. A real friend does not compete; she elicits your rest. A real friend does not diminish; she nurtures growth and inspires courage. A real friend does not help you rationalize; her words take aim with grace.

You cannot hide from the eyes of a real friend. She sees what you hide and hears the words you cannot say. Her prayers for you are priceless treasures as she bends her knees on your behalf.

Praise God for the real friends in your life.

Speaking Truth in Love

Wounds from a friend can be trusted.
PROVERBS 27:6

I would prefer an honest wound from a friend over a hug dipped in malice.

There are times when friends are called to build us up, protect us, or show us our righteousness. This kind of love is easy—to give as well as to receive.

Another kind of love, perhaps even greater due to its rare nature, is tough love. It is meeting us with the solid force of truth when we expect the soft embrace of validation.

Those who know us deeply have the ability to use words with precision and power.

Sometimes the wounds they cause are the only viable method to deflate our pride. Their piercing honesty can lance an infected spirit more quickly than a gentle pomade or frequent bandaging. Be slow to condemn a friend for wounding you. Sometimes the greatest gifts and most teachable moments are inflicted with injury.

GODLY GIRLFRIENDS

*It will be good for you, my daughter, to go with his girls,
because in someone else's field you might be harmed.*

RUTH 2:22

I love the book of Ruth. To me it's a captivating story of romance, redemption, and girl power.

This wonderful biblical book speaks to the value of godly girlfriends. If you have them, praise God. Love and nurture those relationships as though your life depends on them—because it does.

If you do not have a godly group of women with whom to share your heart, pray to the Lord to help you find your nest.

Everything is better when you go with "His girls" . . . Life is safer, more authentic, longer lasting, and just plain more fun. God created women to rely on other women. I am blessed by girlfriends who lift me when I'm low, level me when I'm high, and show me the face of God on a daily basis through their compassion, humor, strength, and unconditional love.

May you cultivate and enjoy the same.

SEEING THE CROSS IN EVERYTHING

You will keep in perfect peace him whose mind
is steadfast, because he trusts in you.

ISAIAH 26:3

❧

I am blessed to have Ann, my spiritual mentor. She visited me, called me, and prayed with me through many of my darker days. She brought this Scripture alive for me with the visual example of looking for the cross in everything. Before a rough mediation session, she told me to find and focus on the cross in the conference room. In preparing for a difficult conversation, she encouraged me to always see the cross in the other person. When the road seemed too long or the hill too steep, she reminded me that the cross is always up ahead of me.

She taught me to ignore and cease assigning value to present circumstances—positive or negative. Circumstances, like feelings, are too unreliable.

The only place to look is at the cross of Jesus—the source of comfort, understanding, and peace—independent of circumstance. He is unchanging and steady. He offers us this same serenity and stability when we make the decision (a choice, not a feeling!) to keep our minds steadfast on Him.

TENDING YOUR GARDEN

Sow for yourselves righteousness, reap the fruit of unfailing love, and break up your unplowed ground.

HOSEA 10:12

When I was finally forced to take a good long look at the topography of my heart, I was appalled. How had I let my garden get into such a state of neglect and disrepair? My inner fields, which once gave me such pleasure as places of promise, growth, and abundance, were ransacked. Everywhere I looked I saw only weeds; hard, rocky soil; and decay. It took a while to get over the shock of my landscape, but eventually I got up and started working.

It's time now to start moving stones, carrying logs, burning debris, and tilling the soil inside. We are told to break up our unplowed ground—the hardened areas in our hearts that cannot be fertile again unless we work them. When you begin, the ache from this hard labor will be refreshing, reminding you of what it's like to feel and to find purpose and pride again in your own garden.

The fruit of unfailing love grows in a field that has been lovingly cultivated with good things like repentance, forgiveness, obedience, and patience. The land within us needs living water, the work of holy hands, and time.

If we work our fields well, we will sustain generations.

Expose Your Sin to Light

This sin will become for you like a high wall, cracked and bulging, that collapses suddenly, in an instant.

ISAIAH 30:13

Spring cleaning for the soul . . . a painful time is a perfect time to take stock of the areas within that need work. If you feel grimy anyway, why not roll up your sleeves and continue to clean in the dark areas of neglect and contamination? If these areas are not purged now, you will never truly be free. Take what you have stuffed in the dark, shake it out, and let it air in the sun. Say the unmentionable, admit instead of rationalize, accept responsibility instead of assigning blame, ask for forgiveness.

The unconfessed sin in your life is a barrier between you and the healing and blessing power of God. Can you feel the pressure behind the barrier, like a dam threatening to burst?

Sin is like that explosion of water—make no mistake about it. If left unmonitored it will break, sweep you into an impossible current, and drown you in its depths.

Rid yourself of the mess; bring your sins to the Lord, and be released into His healing arms.

He is waiting.

A View Without Walls

*O wall of the Daughter of Zion, let
your tears flow like a river.*

LAMENTATIONS 2:18

I used to be a master artisan of the wall. I could construct such a lovely wall, a facade so discreet and deliberate that you would be hard-pressed to tell me where it stopped and I began. Everything looked perfect from outside my wall.

It became a dual source of sin . . . a sin of deception because a wall is false and dividing, and a sin of idolatry because I took pride in my wall, sought safety in it.

When my life started falling apart, shaking at the very core, you can imagine the destruction of my barricade and consequently how exposed I felt. I was forced to come face-to-face with my vulnerability and weakness.

God speaks directly to our walls. He wants to (and will!) break down any barriers that separate Him from His children. No matter what it takes, He wants our true hearts—soft and welcoming—pressed next to Him.

Start tearing down that wall, or expect that He will soon. Let your tears flow like a river to cleanse you and prepare you for the beauty He has in store for you. Without walls, you won't believe the unencumbered view.

OUTSIDE THE BOX

He brought me out into a spacious place; he rescued me because he delighted in me.

2 SAMUEL 22:20

We confine ourselves with our self-made limitations. We fence in our little garden patch and tend to it; meanwhile, the Lord has a vast meadow, streams, fields, and a mountain vista for us.

This place you occupy because you think it is all you can manage or all you deserve is too small for you. The Lord has more in mind, and you will be more of a woman because of it. The Lord delights in you. He wants to rescue you from the way you define yourself so He can define you.

Allow the Lord to draw you out. If you are a wallflower, let Him draw you out of your shell. If you love the spotlight, let Him draw you beyond your ego. If you aren't sure who you are anymore, allow Him to define you properly once and for all. He has a beautiful open space for you, with plenty of room to grow.

SEASONS HAVE LIMITS

*Arise, shine, for your light has come, and
the glory of the Lord rises upon you.*

ISAIAH 60:1

I spent my time in the ashes.

It was a period of my life that was dusty and gray. I love how in Old Testament times, those who were mourning marked their faces with ashes so people understood. They were allotted a specified season of gray, after which they scrubbed up and moved on.

How much healthier is that compared to our society? We put on makeup and a happy face to hide our pain and prohibit people from having compassion and respecting the limits of where we are. We are so busy hiding that we maintain no clear start and stop boundaries on our mourning. We are buried under ashes on the inside.

God will call us to arise out of our ashes and shine when our light has come. Ask God to set your time limit, and be ready to wash up.

THE DOORLESS PRISON

Awake, awake, O Zion, clothe yourself with strength . . .
Shake off your dust; rise up, sit enthroned,
O Jerusalem. Free yourself from the chains on your neck,
O captive Daughter of Zion.

ISAIAH 52:1–2

Wake up, sweetheart! Shake off the layer of dusty disappointment and the cloud of despair. God is calling you to rise up in strength and come find your seat by Him. You are withering away in an open-door prison!

The chains around your neck are heavy and imposing, but they are not attached to anything. Muster all the strength and courage you have, and free yourself from bondage and captivity.

What is holding you here?

What lies have you believed about yourself? What is it that you find so unforgivable? What wound do you have that just will not heal? Ask God to meet you *here,* to heal you *here.*

Invite Him in, and He will come like a great tide and wash you free of dust. He will bear the weight of the chains holding you down. His light will shine brightly on the open door of your self-imposed cell. *Flee. Be free.*

A WITHHOLDING WOMAN

*Do not withhold good from those who deserve it,
when it is in your power to act.*

PROVERBS 3:27

For years when I contemplated the season of Lent, I considered what I should give up.

I thought in terms of my pleasures—wine, coffee, sweets, and Mexican food. Could I really last forty days? Without *coffee*? Really?

One day at church I was struck with a revelation. Maybe I needed to think about the good I didn't do, rather than giving up something "good." I considered the compliments I withheld, the favors I didn't immediately offer, the times I rushed and didn't listen, the embraces from which I refrained, the unspoken words "I love you" and "I forgive you." I decided that each day of Lent I would record an instance or encounter where I sought expression of the good.

I spoke, I listened, and I forgave. I experienced Lent and Easter in fresh and magnificent proportion. Refinement came from offering, not abstaining. My heart split open with the knowledge of all I had withheld.

Lord, open our hearts!

Pass Me Over

He will see the blood . . . and he will not permit the destroyer to enter your houses and strike you down.

EXODUS 12:23

This ancient tale of the first Passover explains how the angel of death visited all the houses in Egypt except those painted in lamb's blood.

The same is true today. The enemy prowls around like a lion, looking for someone to devour. When he sees a person or a home that is "covered" in the blood of the Lamb Jesus, he moves on. He would much rather find easy prey than mess with one who belongs to the Lord. Just like a robber would prefer someone who is unaware of her surroundings, not paying attention, and appears weak, the enemy will choose his victim based on what seems like a sure thing. We can make him look elsewhere.

Pray to cover your home and loved ones with the applied blood of Jesus. Think of the lengths He went to, and all that He endured on our behalf. This blood symbolizes all our freedom and all our protection.

Let's use it.

What Do You Stand For?

Blessed is the man who does not condemn
himself by what he approves.

ROMANS 14:22

Perhaps this is an ancient version of the modern cliché "You have to stand for something or you will fall for anything."

We approve of things and people in two ways—actively and passively. We actively approve, agreeing verbally or non-verbally, by aligning our actions. We passively approve by doing nothing—showing no disagreement and no contrary action.

The same can be said about our reaction to sin or evil. Sin is a dark and slippery thing. We are called to take a stand against it. Of course, we don't feel as if we literally approve of poor choices in our own lives, or in the lives of other people. But often our silence or our lack of resistance amounts to tacit approval, and this is very dangerous.

In order to make progress in our spiritual lives, we must clarify our boundaries and find the courage to speak our convictions. Make sure your approval means something, because you wield an opposing force in contrast.

CULTIVATING A REFLEX RESPONSE

Be strong in the Lord and in his mighty power.
EPHESIANS 6:10

Memorize this verse and hide it in your heart.

When I start to falter, my first reaction is a panicky, "Oh, no! What do I do?" No matter how long I have spent in the workshop, my progress is made evident only in the initial moment of peril. We prepare ourselves internally to meet the challenges externally. We rehearse in advance so our responses are involuntary when the moment of truth arrives.

There isn't one situation, one temptation, or one question that cannot be answered correctly by the response "Be strong in the Lord and in His mighty power." On a multiple-choice test, this is answer (d) All of the above. Use this verse to steady yourself in shaky moments until you regain your stability in the Rock.

God is not telling you to be tough on your own, or to come up with the right thing to do. He is saying to rely on His power and His strength, and allow Him to do for you what He knows is best.

ANCHOR OF HOPE

We have this hope as an anchor for the soul,
firm and secure. It enters the inner sanctuary
behind the curtain, where Jesus, who went before us,
has entered on our behalf.

HEBREWS 6:19–20

How easily our souls are tossed about in waves of uncertainty and tides of circumstance. We are so insignificant out in open water. We are such vulnerable creatures when we rely on our own survival and navigation tactics. But an anchor, firmly and expertly tethered, will keep the boat steady regardless of high seas. Remember, waves are on the surface, and the anchor sits calmly on a deeper level.

Our hope in the Lord anchors the tiny, weather-beaten crafts of our souls. Our hope keeps us in the right spot regardless of how impossible it seems to navigate during a storm. Sometimes a storm is no time to try to navigate at all, but a time to get still.

This hope permeates us, through all our many walls and complicated layers. Jesus cuts through all of that like a hot knife through frosting. He goes directly to the secret, sacred places and ministers to us there by reconciling us to God.

BOUNDARIES ARE OF GOD

Simply let your "Yes" be "Yes," and your "No,"
"No"; anything beyond this comes from the evil one.
MATTHEW 5:37

A major part of starting over and learning to be a good steward of our time and our hearts is to establish good boundaries.

Where we have clear direction from the Lord, there is always immediate relief . . . no dissonance, no stress, no desire to reconsider. We are instantly free and empowered to pursue the things that are God's will for us.

Indecision and unclear boundaries are not from the Lord. They give a foothold to the enemy, a place for him to gain advantage by default. They cause us to dilute our yes, which compromises our sincerity and our impact.

If you aren't sure what God wants, take your time! Be clear about your intent. Think before you speak. Pray before you commit one second of your time or one ounce of passion from your heart. Align yourself with God, and give your words power to define the life you want.

Yes or no?

A VISION WORTH FIGHTING FOR

*It is God who arms me with strength and makes
my way perfect . . . He trains my hands for battle;
my arms can bend a bow of bronze. You give me
your shield of victory, and your right hand
sustains me; you stoop down to make me great.*

PSALM 18:32–35

The battle that is waging right now is not one of lawyers, flying papers, and dueling conference rooms. It has far greater implications for you than that.

In the spiritual realm, daily decisions you make now build upon one another to become the life you will live later, long after this season is behind you. The battle is the fight for your heart and soul. Will you allow your heart to close . . . to become cold and barren? Or will you allow the Lord to train you to fight to keep your heart open, free, and victorious?

Ask the Lord to treat you to a glimpse of His vision for your life. Hold on to that beauty and do not forsake it at any cost. It is the one and only battle that is worth the fight.

Train and be ready. He will stoop down to make you great.

Rise Up!

So do not throw away your confidence;
it will be richly rewarded.

HEBREWS 10:35

I remember days when I wanted to hide.

When it all seemed like more than I could manage, considering the emotional bricks I was carrying in my invisible backpack. I wanted to pull my baseball cap low in the grocery store and not see anyone. I wanted no part of my former confident, energetic, happy persona. I felt like that woman was long gone.

It is in those precise moments, in those exact spots, where we need to rise up. We need to cultivate confidence in Christ when our own self-images are shot. When our own egos are pierced and deflated, confidence in Christ proves unshakable and independent of circumstance.

Ask the Lord to build you up, to strengthen your resolve, to help you rise above present conditions. Do not throw away your confidence—it isn't dead.

Resuscitate it with the breath of the Holy Spirit.

THIS WON'T STICK

The Lord your God is the one who goes with you to fight for you against your enemies to give you victory.

DEUTERONOMY 20:4

Think of yourself as coated in spiritual Teflon.

Things might get hot. Things might get sticky. Things might get messy. In fact, they probably already have. But nothing that comes over you can harm you. Nothing that touches you will stick. Whatever transpires can and will be washed away. In a relatively short period of time, you will not clearly recall how you felt today. Why? Because it cannot stick. You are passing through this trial, not stuck here. This pain is a detour, not a destiny.

You are completely protected and built to last when you allow God to fight your battles for you. Turn your struggles over to Him. Holy blood has already been shed to ensure your safety. The end of your story is intact.

The next time things heat up, think of Teflon. You are already victorious, and you are never exposed or alone.

Keep your eyes on the cross, not the loss.

D-DAY

They confronted me in the day of my disaster,
but the Lord was my support.

2 SAMUEL 22:19

We all dread that moment. When the phone rings in the middle of the night, when your nervous spouse wants to have a serious talk, when your child's teacher calls, or when a policeman appears at your front door . . . these things don't usually portend good news.

Eventually, if you live long enough, you will be "confronted in the day of your disaster." The moment or phone call you have been dreading is suddenly upon you. In that instant you are forced to face your fear. There isn't time to call your friend or prepare yourself—the moment overtakes you.

Other years of your life are the workshop for moments like this. Your response or your gut instinct in that second can be prepared only by daily spiritual training.

In the moment of your disaster, the Lord is your support. Train yourself to look to Him first, and you will be ready.

SAFE IN HIS COMPANY

*"They will fight against you but will not overcome
you, for I am with you and will rescue you,"
declares the Lord.*

JEREMIAH 1:19

I went through a dark period plagued by nightmares, insomnia, and an inability to eat. I felt constantly under attack as even the simplest tasks were met with unholy resistance.

When someone finally explained to me that I wasn't crazy and that spiritual warfare was real, I wanted to get strong and fight back. I wanted a good life and refused to accept that this was my new reality. Shortly after that, things started to turn around. I prayed for protection before bed each night, and the nightmares lessened and finally stopped entirely. I slept peacefully.

I began running so that I could get strong, and my appetite returned. The Lord helped me break the chains that were holding me back. He fought for me and rescued me. Though I slipped and fell hard, I was not overcome. And you won't be either!

INESCAPABLE REFORM

We will all be changed.
1 CORINTHIANS 15:51

We cannot escape trials. We cannot hide from seasons of refinement. We cannot delay our destinies. We cannot push back against the tide of circumstances.

God has a plan for each one of us, and we are swept up into it.

He intimately knows the work we need to do on ourselves, because He programmed our potential. He also knows exactly what must and will happen in our lives to bring about the required change. He knows the variance between who we are now and who and what we are meant to be and do according to His wise design. C. S. Lewis explained that we will reach maturity one of two ways, through either experience or discipline. We can pursue discipline and acquire the wisdom assigned to this trial, or we can experience another and still another trial until we finally grasp the lesson.

We can make it easy on ourselves and surrender. Or we can resist and do it the hard way. Regardless, one thing is certain:

We will all be changed.

TRIALS BUILD CHARACTER

If you do not stand firm in your faith,
you will not stand at all.

ISAIAH 7:9

Tough times reveal who you are.

You will not find yourself in times of success because you are too caught up in yourself and your things.

You will not find yourself in ordinary times because you are too complacent and too restless.

God permits pain and suffering for reasons only He knows. But we can understand this much: hard times reveal our true nature. Suffering strips our character of weak and meaningless sediment and exposes only the necessary, strong, and authentic parts of who we are. At this point we truly have something to offer the world. We no longer have to pretend to have depth and endurance. Perhaps God can use you to help someone who is suffering through a broken marriage. Perhaps Gods wants you to be an example to your children. Perhaps God is calling you to even be a testimony to your ex!

Stand firm in your faith to prevail in a season of trial.

Obedience Rooted in Love

*Live as free men, but do not use your freedom
as a cover-up for evil.*

1 PETER 2:16

Since the beginning, as evidenced in the garden, God has given His children free will. We have the option to choose Him (life) or not choose Him (death).

Our freedom is a gift. It ensures that our obedience is based in love, not a mandate. But our gift of choice is not without risk, nor is it an opportunity for a moral free-for-all. Instead, it is a chance to become disciplined and well-trained through exercising our right to decide for ourselves.

This notion of discipline is not intended to be suffocating or boring. To the contrary, when we abide by God's principles we experience a rush of true freedom that is more exciting than any temporary thrill of sin. The pain of a broken relationship could become a foothold for excusing rebellious behavior. Now more than ever, it is crucial to behave in a way that honors God and preserves His protection and provision.

No Loopholes

Has he not made with me an everlasting covenant,
arranged and secured in every part?

2 SAMUEL 23:5

A covenant goes far beyond our understanding of a binding document. There are no loopholes or statutes of limitations. Every "i" is dotted; every "t" is crossed. Every detail, every possible scenario, is planned for, arranged, and secured in every part. It is unchangeable and everlasting.

When a marriage ends, it is easy to lose faith in the concept of commitment. Commitment means that you will stay when you feel like leaving. Feelings are supposed to be irrelevant in commitment. However, the problem is not with commitment; it's with people. We are frail and we fail. We can study covenant relationships to learn more about commitment from God's perspective.

The kind of relationship you have with the Lord is a covenant relationship. His promises are ironclad. You can read the Bible to better understand this covenant. You will find hundreds of personal promises, from God to you, to ensure your redemption, your salvation, your healing, your forgiveness, and your future.

These promises are yours to claim. They are held in your name, arranged and secured in every part.

KNOW HIS VOICE

He who has been stealing must steal no longer.
EPHESIANS 4:28

There is a war within. Anyone who tells you otherwise is blind. Perhaps Jesus identified Satan as a thief because he has a cunning ability to deceive. He can disguise himself so well that believers often have trouble discerning the origin of thoughts, voices, or instruction.

We need to pray for discernment and clarity. When we aren't certain, we need to condition ourselves to stop, listen carefully, and ask for confirmation. We need to know the Savior's voice, intimately. We need to intuit His instruction at the level of an almost imperceptible nudge. We can develop this discernment by spending regular time in prayer and Bible study. Through that process we are able to hear His voice and experience the fullness of life that He promises.

FIND THE COURAGE TO BE REAL

Do not give way to fear.
1 PETER 3:6

We make many decisions each day that lead us either on a path of authenticity or away from our true selves. Small details make the difference, like the way we truthfully answer a question or if we stop to listen instead of continuing on in a rush.

The biggest barrier to being our truest selves is fear.

It's a risk to be real. What if I offer myself and I am rejected? What if I speak what's on my heart and I am judged, or ridiculed? What if I opt for love in a difficult situation and I am denied? What if I try and I am met with what I perceive as failure? What if I extend forgiveness only to be injured again? These things are not our concern; we are called to be real and to be brave. We have the unfailing love of Jesus Christ, so we are not to be mastered by fear.

We have been promised perfect rest in Him, which crowds out doubt. Take the chance.

PERFECT IN IMPERFECTION

Love comes from God.
1 JOHN 4:7

I admit, for a while I was angry at love.

I thought love wasn't all it was cracked up to be. It didn't last. It wasn't worth it. The deeper it went, the more it hurt. Love was irrational, complicated, elusive, and unreliable. And I was done with it.

Little by little the Lord healed my heart. My anger toward love began to fade.

Now I'm beginning to see that love is perfect because it comes from God; in fact, it is God. It's just humanity that scars and strangles love and mars its perfection. Because love comes from God it is worth it, whatever the cost. No matter what damage has been done in the name of love, we are incomplete without it.

Only love can heal and restore where love has been lost.

Loving well is our highest calling. Being loved well is our greatest gift.

Desire Is Not Enough

I found that the very commandment that was intended to bring life actually brought death. For sin, seizing the opportunity afforded by the commandment, deceived me.

ROMANS 7:10–11

Think of the red alarm button in elevators. It is always the button my children try to push. I have thought of doing it myself. Why? For no other reason than we are not supposed to. It's red. It stands out. It's right there next to all the other benign buttons.

The same idea applies to sin and the laws proclaiming what we are not supposed to do. Simply stating the prohibition incites curiosity and rebellion. This strange phenomenon comes from the enemy, not from God. Sin is deceptive above all else.

With this in mind, we now understand why changing our behavior (and ultimately our character) requires a change of heart through Christ and the Holy Spirit, not merely a willfulness to adhere to the rules.

Just as in a good marriage, desire alone is not sufficient because it eventually wanes. Love is what leads to obedience and lasting improvement.

ALWAYS A BRIDE

I will betroth you to me forever; I will betroth you in righteousness and justice, in love and compassion.

HOSEA 2:19

❧

Marriage is between two humans and therefore fallible. The word *betrothal* is the word used most often to talk about the relationship between a husband and a wife or a man and a woman engaged to be married.

This is the relationship God wants to have with you . . . as passionate, as devoted, as committed, as honorable, as intimate as the finest of married couples. His fidelity will never fail you, He is incapable of breaking promises, He loves you with increasing depth and dedication from moment to moment, He is unmatched in His ability to handle your heart and your emotions with tenderness and intuition.

He Himself is righteousness and justice; He personifies love and compassion. And He wants you to be His bride, to love and cherish forever.

It's natural to lament the death of a marriage, but in our grief let us not lose sight of our appreciation for the fact that we are still betrothed, still desired, still vital to the one Being who will never fail us.

You Will Push Through This

I consider that our present sufferings are not worth comparing with the glory that will be revealed in us.

ROMANS 8:18

Think of the suffering and pain of labor during childbirth.

In that moment, you can think of nothing other than breathing through the agony of each contraction. There is a primal and simple goal . . . relief. Labor is suffering; it is tearing, swearing, blood, and sweat. It is humbling in a very primitive way.

And yet, later, when you talk to a mother she will show off photos and tell you all kinds of stories about her children. Labor, which was so intense and enormous at the time, is a vague memory. The pain is completely meaningless compared to the joy of motherhood. It is nothing compared to the sweet honor of raising a child.

Relate this example to your present situation. Consider that something beautiful is being born through the labor in your life right now, and realize that God has an eternal, glorious home for you that will make this life's sufferings seem like a vapor.

THE EMPATHY OF CHRIST

*The Lord is close to the brokenhearted and
saves those who are crushed in spirit.*

PSALM 34:18

We all have spent desperate hours in our personal gardens of Gethsemane. When a marriage fails, we undoubtedly experience heartache that feels like we could weep tears of blood. In these desperate moments, when we feel the profound sense of being lost, we are ironically the closest to being found.

At our deepest hours of despair, Jesus can reach out to us and bring healing and peace to our souls because He experienced a far greater betrayal and abandonment.

Unlike His human disciples, He will not sleep, abandon us, or disown us in the garden. Instead, because He is no stranger to suffering, He comes to us when others prefer to shrink back. He embraces us in our misery with pierced arms, understanding agony, and comforting us with His eternal perspective of blessing that is waiting on the other side.

SUSTAINING LOVE

[The Lord] will quiet you with his love.
ZEPHANIAH 3:17

I prayed so hard for my marriage to be restored that I thought God would respond positively if for no other reason than my sheer persistence alone. I thought that if I could only convey to God how hard I was fighting for my family, He would grant me its restoration. My efforts did not impress God; in fact, He finally took notice of me when I relinquished the fight and prayed for His will alone, nothing more.

Sometimes we pray so hard for something that we forget why we wanted it so badly in the first place. I know God always answers prayer, but it's His timing that tests my faith and my patience.

Even if, as in my case, the answer is a loving and firm "no," He does not leave me alone with that "no." When He does not grant us our wishes, He will quiet our hearts without them. The cracks remaining in the aftermath of "no" are spackled expertly.

He does not want to quiet you with a blessing; He wants to quiet you with Himself.

A MENDED FAMILY

From him the whole body, joined and held together
by every supporting ligament, grows and builds
itself up in love, as each part does its work.

EPHESIANS 4:16

Paul was referring to the church in his beautiful analogy of the human body. When each part is healthy, functioning properly, and growing consistently, the body can do amazing things.

I like to continue this analogy by applying it to my family. In the same way, as we maintain our health, nourishment, and functionality, we grow and work together in love. When one person leaves a family, there is a period of healing and limited function and joy. But like a real body, we mend, adapt, and find new ways to do things and new ways to find joy.

When I look at my family now, I see how the Lord has filled an empty spot with His love and made us stronger, happier, more cohesive, and faith-filled than we were before. I wouldn't have believed it to be possible, yet here we are.

Thank You, God, for my family.

THE VERDICT ON DIVORCE

*The Lord is acting as the witness between you
and the wife of your youth, because you have broken
faith with her, though she is your partner,
the wife of your marriage covenant. Has not the Lord
made them one? In flesh and spirit they are his . . .
"I hate divorce," says the Lord God of Israel.*

MALACHI 2:14–16

Wow.

Okay, so if you had any confusion about the Lord's feelings on divorce, read that one again. He is crystal clear.

The reason divorce hurts so badly and feels so awful is because it is wrong. It is not what God ever intended for us. So if you are feeling angry and if you hate divorce too, it's okay, you are in good company.

But the comfort here is in the words "The Lord is acting as the witness between you and the wife of your youth." This means you are not alone. This means there is Someone else present who is watching and tending to details. He is right in the thick of it with you, intending to carry you to a better place.

He wants you to have a marriage covenant, one that is a rope bound of three cords . . . you (improved and able to keep a covenant), Himself, and a godly man who respects the covenant issued in faith. The Lord can redeem any situation in His time.

THE LADY OF THE HOUSE

*By wisdom a house is built, and through
understanding it is established.*

PROVERBS 24:3

You don't need a husband to be the head of the household.
That role is one you should now embrace and develop. Your
circumstances offer an opportunity to rise to a new challenge.
It isn't a choice of whether or not you will do it, but how you
will do it. You might as well do it exceptionally well.

Perhaps you never thought you could run a house, care
for children, be the spiritual leader, manage finances, make
a living, find your calling, and create a peaceful and envi-
able life all on your own. Well, you aren't on your own. You
have God with you, enabling you to do it all with grace.

In fact, it's time now to be a far greater woman than
you previously believed you could be. You can step confidently and courageously into this role. Give your house to
Jesus, and proclaim it a house of the Lord! Make choices
prayerfully, purposefully, and bravely. If children are
depending on you, you have all the more reason to love
powerfully and stand tall.

ASCENDING FROM THE PIT

[The Lord] lifted me out of the slimy pit,
out of the mud and mire; he set my feet
on a rock and gave me a firm place to stand.

PSALM 40:2

My slimy pit was slippery with deceit and tabloids, photographers and garden-variety gossip. I was a conversation-stopper at preschool, and I despised the checkout line at the grocery store. When I look back on those times, now instead of cringing, I marvel at how far God has brought me from them.

Trying to claw my way out of the pit got me absolutely nowhere. I would simply exhaust myself and slump, defeated and dejected, back into the mud and mire. My own efforts were futile. A wise woman said to me in a soft voice from the edge of the pit, "I can't tell you it will never be this bad again, but I can tell you that for the rest of your life you will know what to do. Come on, let's pray."

When I quit thrashing and floundering in the gunk and quieted my spirit enough to begin to listen and trust, the mud and mire began to dry. I saw footholds I hadn't seen and I began my ascent from the pit.

The Lord truly lifted me, gave me a path and the courage for climbing. He set my feet upon a rock.

Every single entry in this devotional is a tribute and a thank-you note to God.

Now you know what to do. Let's pray.

SHARING HOPE

Always be prepared to give an answer to everyone who asks you to give the reason for the hope that you have.
1 PETER 3:15

When you have been to the bottom and begin your ascent from the pit, your hope will increase in proportion to your elevation. You will begin to see new possibilities where you saw nothing before. You will feel something inside you that you may not recognize at first—excitement.

Once you grasp the idea that the Lord is carrying you, having a second chance suddenly sounds thrilling. You will see new possibilities when you realize that He is with you, taking your burdens. A Christian life is a hopeful life, and you have many things to look forward to. Over time this pain will become just a part of your story, not your whole life. As your outlook begins to change in response to the changes in your heart, many things will open up for you.

People will notice this change in you. They might directly or indirectly ask about this new you. This is the opportunity to give credit where credit is due. Give thanks to the Lord by sharing your faith, which is the reason for the hope you have.

A Bigger Story to Tell

*You will receive power when the Holy Spirit
comes on you; and you will be my witnesses . . .
to the ends of the earth.*

ACTS 1:8

It may not feel like it today, but you will get through this time. You will overcome this season with grace, courage, and class. You will more than survive, you will thrive.

You won't get through this on your own, however. You will receive power from the Holy Spirit. The Holy Spirit will guide your decision making and give you a brave spirit to carve out a new and better life.

And after this season is behind you, that same power will inspire you to tell people about the Lord and His mighty power. You may or may not need to use words. Your courage, your steadfastness to your faith, the open status of your heart, and your unaltered ability to keep on loving will be a case study for Christ.

Everything you do and say matters because this is no longer just your story. Be diligent.

SINGLED OUT

*Consider it pure joy, my brothers, whenever
you face trials of many kinds.*

JAMES 1:2

Trials contain fear, disappointment, loss, pain, or, at the very least, a season of discomfort and doubt. Why, then, am I supposed to consider this "pure joy"? How much Prozac would that take anyway?

The joy is in this: God has singled you out amid the masses as a worthy subject for refinement. The Creator of the universe sees something in you He can use for His glory! He is working on you to get you to a place to give and receive blessings on a higher scale. This is the testing of your faith; your time in the fire to be purified and strengthened.

In the same way a boss in the workplace gives you assignments to groom you for a promotion, the Lord has greater work in mind for you than what you used to do. You may not like the current assignment, but your job is to do it well and without complaint so you can move on.

This may not be the attention you had in mind, but it is exactly the attention you need.

A HEAVENLY REVERSAL

*You intended to harm me, but God intended
it for good to accomplish what is now being done,
the saving of many lives.*

GENESIS 50:20

There isn't one trial, one fiery dart, or one bad day of which God is unaware. The enemy of your soul, which can lurk around you in human form as well, does intend to weaken you, to use you, or to take advantage of you. But don't let this frighten you. There is Someone much bigger than you, and much, much stronger than the one who intends to harm you.

He will protect you and initiate an unbelievable reversal.

He will take every single thing aimed against you and turn it for good. He will bring lightness and blessing into your life, and He will use your experiences to transform you. He will prepare you for work far greater than you ever imagined you could accomplish. He will use your pain, your loneliness, your healing, and your compassion to save many lives, *yours included.*

Banquet Proportions

The thief comes only to steal and kill and destroy; I have come that they may have life, and have it to the full.

JOHN 10:10

Humanity's story on earth is epic, set against a backdrop of history and the timeless battleground of good and evil. Since the Garden of Eden, the thief has wreaked havoc on our earthly lives. We cannot escape the consequences of pain, or loss in a sinful world. But Jesus offers a way out. He tells us to expect trials, but He also tells us to take heart because He has overcome the world.

He not only wants us to have life, but He wants us to live fully, abundantly, and peacefully. This promise applies to eternal life as well as to life today, right now. He wants us to have life to the full! Can you see how much you are loved?

We aren't called to feign satisfaction in meager scraps; we are called to join the Lord at a banquet table and dine like a daughter of the Most High.

PACE YOURSELF

Let us run with perseverance the race marked out for us.
HEBREWS 12:1

I belong to a women's running group, and we often run pacing workouts on the local high school track. After warming up we begin a series of 5 one-mile repeats. Each mile is four laps around the track. The goal is to remain at a consistent speed or run a negative split, which means to run faster at the end than when you started.

It's tempting to start too fast in the false exuberance of fresh legs and be unable to complete the work. It's easy to be inconsistent, speeding up or slowing down depending on who is running nearby, or whether the coach is watching.

I love the metaphor of the track as I apply it to my life.

We are called spiritually to run our own race, to persevere, to be nourished, to be consistent, to set goals, to remain focused, and to push our limits.

I want to mature in my faith to a state of tenacity and sinew. I want to know my pace and to gain the experience, endurance, and wisdom to run a lifetime negative split.

FULL OF GOD

[Jesus] must become greater; I must become less.
JOHN 3:30

It embarrasses me deeply to admit that there was a time in my life when I had no room for God.

I was filled with ego, busyness, material things, and bubbles of emptiness. I was climbing and spinning, going nowhere in many directions at once. I have very few solid memories of this time. My priorities were so out of whack that I didn't "have time" to pray or connect with God. Fleeting attempts to get to church do not equate with having a spiritual life. I remember feeling fraudulent on holidays fraught with religious meaning and richness, yet vaguely hollow for me. As hard as I tried, I could not bridge the gap I had allowed within my own soul.

I thought I could do and have it all. Until, like an old cartoon where the safe plummets out the window to the sidewalk below, I was hit hard; flattened by the weight of it all.

Now I want to be full of God, not full of myself.

Beyond Our Vision

*Now faith is being sure of what we hope for
and certain of what we do not see.*

HEBREWS 11:1

The catalyst to God's healing, redemption, and favor is faith. And here we have a precise definition of a seemingly elusive concept.

We must consciously cultivate an atmosphere and attitude of faith. We must live in hopeful expectancy that regardless of circumstance or feelings, God is in the process of turning things around. Divorce has the potential to build or erode our faith. We can look at the wreckage around us and give in to feelings of futility, or we can have an outlook of faith and believe that God is busy behind the scenes, making something lasting and beautiful out of the debris.

Everything we can see will eventually turn to dust. Our only true reliance is in the unseen—the only thing that never changes, never fails, and never disappoints.

Faith is a choice. Faith is a deliberate decision to look to God and confidently expect Him to deliver on our behalf.

LET HIM LOVE YOU

I will search for the lost and bring back the strays.
I will bind up the injured and strengthen the weak.
EZEKIEL 34:16

Do you see how loved you are? Do you feel how pursued you are? How desired you are? How protected you are? How coddled you are?

Let the Son of God come for you.
Let Him replace your missing pieces.
Let Him heal your brokenness.
Let Him cure your afflictions.

Where other eyes choose blindness, God's eyes seek until He finds. As far as you run away, He will find you and bring you home. As chipped and misshapen as your heart is, He will smooth the cracks. As sick as you may be, or as dark as your warped world of sin has become, He comes with His healing light to lead you to safety.

There is no gap larger than His love can bridge. No failure that He cannot redeem. No plague of spirit He cannot cure. Stop running and hiding, and allow Him to love you back to health.

AN ETERNAL GARDEN

All men are like grass, and all their glory is like the flowers of the field; the grass withers and the flowers fall, but the word of the Lord stands forever.

1 PETER 1:24–25

Seasons change, landscapes alter, blooms fade, petals fall. Whatever earthly pursuit you relish or human form you revere, know that they all amount to the same dust. If all men wither like grass, then we must learn to keep our earthly relationships in proper perspective. The only lasting relationship is with the Lord.

The success, status, and glory of this world are insignificant blips on the face of eternity.

Only God's word (His love and promises) stands the test of time. When everything else falls away, the Lord remains, unshakable and unalterable.

If you are going to trust a promise, be sure it is one of His.

If you are going to believe in something, make sure it is the one and only thing that will not fail you. When God's words paint the backdrop of your mind, you can be sure the landscape will be beautiful for all seasons. Spend your time tending what will last.

SEE FOR YOURSELF

*First take the plank out of your own eye,
and then you will see clearly to remove the
speck from your brother's eye.*

MATTHEW 7:5

In other words, mind your own business!

Jesus is telling us that we have more than enough work to do on ourselves, which should leave little time or energy for judging others. He prefers we leave judgment to the only one qualified—Himself.

Our own sins and weaknesses blind us, rendering us unable to see ourselves clearly. The very thing that annoys us about others, or provokes a spirit of judgment, is most likely the area that we need to work on. Notice the size difference between a speck and a plank. God is telling us that our own issues are more problematic. We need to first seek Him to clear our own vision. Only then, in plain view of our own weaknesses, can we offer any real assistance to others. When you feel a twinge of judgment, realize that it is illuminating something you need to see about yourself.

WE CAN'T EVEN IMAGINE

No eye has seen, no ear has heard, no mind has conceived what God has prepared for those who love him.

1 CORINTHIANS 2:9

There are many false and temporary ways to try to cheer yourself up. You can eat too much ice cream, read too many self-help books, spend too much money shopping, or exercise to excess. You can look to other people to lift your spirits and rely on them to keep you lifted, much to their annoyance and exhaustion.

The world offers many beautifully written greeting cards that hold sweet sentiments. But these words in 1 Corinthians are an exquisite balm to the soul.

These words tell us that as grand as we can sweep our expectations, as broad as we can stretch our horizons, as fanciful as we can loose our imaginations, it is all nothing compared to the good God has planned for us.

Our own personal notion of the end-all, be-all, too-good-to-be-true scenario doesn't even register on His blessing spectrum.

Do you feel protected? Cherished? Loved? Excited?

You should.

You have no idea.

The Catalyst of Faith

But the message they heard was of no value to them,
because those who heard did not combine it with faith.

HEBREWS 4:2

૨૭

Alka Seltzer without water—no fizz.
Oxygen without hydrogen—no water.
Flour without yeast—no bread.
Seed without sunshine—no flower.
Blue without yellow—no green.
Relationship without trust—no friendship.
Egg without sperm—no baby.
Spark without air—no flame.

Without specific catalysts, certain results can never be achieved. In order to make spiritual progress, it is not enough to simply read the Bible or sit in church and listen to sermons. The activating ingredient to our understanding is faith.

After we hear God's message, we must act upon it with our faith. Perhaps you are experiencing bitterness or anger as a result of a failed relationship. You have heard God's declarations to put those emotions behind you, but you lack the determination to do so. Let me encourage you to trust God's word and act in faith. His promises will bloom in your life if you activate your faith in Him.

The Power of Praise

O Lord, God of heaven, the great and awesome God . . .
let your ear be attentive and your eyes open
to hear the prayer your servant is praying.

NEHEMIAH 1:5–6

We must approach God by acknowledging His excellence and praising His power. Praise paves the way for prayers to be heard, and patience provides the return route for God's response.

Either God says yes to our requests, or in His no He tells us to wait and trust because He has something better in mind for us. Even His no has a loving measure of yes.

Regardless of the perceived fruitfulness of our prayer lives, faith assures us that our prayers are always heard. Keep telling God how great and awesome He is. Frame your communication in thanksgiving. Instead of, "God, give me guidance on how to handle this situation," you can say, "Father, I thank You that You have everything under control and will guide my every step." The more you praise Him, the more open you become to receiving discernment and direction.

Praise releases you into a state of gratitude by reminding you of how much He has *already done.*

BEWARE THE COLD SHOULDER

My days have passed, my plans are shattered,
and so are the desires of my heart.

JOB 17:11

Who knows more about brokenness than Job? Job lost every single good thing in his life, except his faith. He was stripped of his fortune, his family, his friends, and his health. From the depths of despair, he still would not curse God.

Instead, Job talked to God. He expressed his pain, his illness, and his emptiness. He grieved his loss openly, never shutting God out.

We have a choice either to include God in our pain, or to exclude Him and try to make it on our own. Because of Job's strength in the face of testing and the fact that nothing could cause him to deny God, God blessed Job many times over and restored his life.

Be wary that your pain does not cause you to give God the cold shoulder.

SEEK HIGHER GROUND

If sinners entice you, do not give in to them.
PROVERBS 1:10

It's easy to be misled by people who know your weaknesses and to revert back to familiar patterns. People who knew the old you prefer to keep you defined by the old you. It makes them feel better about their own rationalization or lack of progress, and it eliminates the need to understand why and how you have changed. We cannot escape the temptations of the world, nor can we defeat them through our own strength.

Choosing to walk with God is a series of choices. It is submitting, every day, over and over, remaining in a holy state of dependence at all times. We don't have to fight the enemy of sin. We merely need to resist him and allow the Lord to fight on our behalf.

We will never be tempted beyond what we can handle; we will always be given an escape route. Watch for the exit signs and be ready to move.

LET HIM FIGHT FOR YOU

Do not be afraid of any man,
for judgment belongs to God.
DEUTERONOMY 1:17

It's easy to become fearful when your former lover and best friend is suddenly cast as your adversary. Harsh words spoken during this difficult time can do lasting damage. Hasty actions can lead to regret.

Stop fighting for the sake of fighting and let God take up for you. Watch how He puts the puzzle together with pieces you thought were missing. Notice how He protects you and gives you wisdom when you thought everything was hopeless. When you are tempted to lash out, a response based in fear, turn the hot, bubbling mass of emotion over to the Lord instead.

Leave judgment to Him. Take courage and find steadiness in the Word of God from the Old Testament and *do not be afraid of any man.*

ACE THIS TEST

*The Lord your God is testing you to find out whether
you love him with all your heart and with all your soul.*
DEUTERONOMY 13:3

The answer to this test is a matter of trust.

The way we show the Lord whether or not we love Him with all our heart and soul is to surrender ourselves and our lives into His hands.

The more we know God, the more we trust Him. The more we trust Him, the greater our faith. How do we get to know God? We pray to Him, seeking Him and sharing our hearts with Him. We read His Word, allowing Him to speak to us in His timeless and profound method. We offer what we have and ask Him to multiply it and direct us.

It isn't so much a matter of effort as it is a matter of release. It is an infinitely more challenging task because it requires giving up our control and self-reliance. It is letting go of the small to hold on to something big.

When the Lord allows a season of testing in your life, show Him the depth of your love by placing your trust in Him.

NOT ENOUGH ON OUR OWN

Though one may be overpowered, two can defend themselves. A cord of three strands is not quickly broken.
ECCLESIASTES 4:12

If you have ever been in a good relationship, you know the deep importance of intimacy. We were created to need each other. Our achievements mean nothing if we have no one to share them with. When a relationship fails, we experience profound loneliness.

This verse offers the key to maintaining a successful relationship. In any friendship, partnership, or marriage, when we have Jesus in both our hearts we have a cord of three strands. We need to be more intentional about inviting Jesus into our time spent with friends, and ultimately we need Him as a permanent part of a threesome in marriage. We need a third party to referee, bridge any communication gaps, break any tie on an impasse, and make up for all the ways we fail each other. He is the one who takes our meager offerings in a relationship and works His loaves and fishes magic to make sure everyone is nourished and satisfied.

From my perspective now, I cannot see how a marriage can endure without the constant presence of Christ at its core.

FREEDOM IN THE FLOCK

The Lord is my shepherd; I shall not be in want.

PSALM 23:1

I love the image of Christ as the Good Shepherd. There is an Episcopal church near my house with a beautiful sculpture of Christ tenderly holding a little lamb. I like it when the traffic light is red and I have a moment to stare at this scene. I often think about the relationship between the Shepherd and His lambs.

Sheep don't worry about anything. They have everything provided for them—food, water, protection, and shelter. They know and trust the voice of their shepherd and live freely and happily as he tends to them.

We, too, have all these things because we have a Good Shepherd to care for us. He provides for and protects His flock. The only voice we need to know in times of trouble is His.

Reflect on Jesus holding a little lamb. Think of how much easier life could be if we just stuck together and trusted more deeply in His care.

MAKING THE MOST OF FREE WILL

I have set before you life and death, blessings and curses.
Now choose life, so that you and your children may live.
DEUTERONOMY 30:19

Since the days of Eden, we have been granted the power of choice. We can choose to live under the umbrella of God's protection and provision or to step outside and try it on our own.

Accepting our salvation is a choice. We choose to invite the Holy Spirit to dwell within us; He does not force His way into our hearts. Accepting God's law is a choice. We can choose to live a life of obedience; God wants us to follow out of love, not coercion. Accepting freedom and forgiveness is a choice. Just because a gift is handed to us, we are not forced to unwrap it. Accepting our circumstances is a choice. We can fight the reality of where we are, or we can progress more quickly by making the best of things right now.

We are instructed to choose life. That is not a onetime choice; it's a daily choice, an hourly choice, a moment-by-moment diversion of thinking. Decisions big and small point to life, or point away. What a gift to have a fine mind, and the freedom to use it well.

IMPROVING OUR TEST SCORES

*We are not trying to please men but God,
who tests our hearts.*

1 THESSALONIANS 2:4

One day I said more than I should have in a conversation, and it came back to haunt me. It was a painful lesson in escalation, and in learning the art of discretion and the value of a closed mouth.

The Lord varies the degrees of getting our attention, beginning with a gentle tap on the shoulder and progressing to a thump on the head, or a full-blown face plant. Instead of "Why me?" what if our immediate response became, "Yes, Lord, You have my full attention. What would You like me to learn here?"

If we could just learn to submit when we feel like panicking! We would greatly reduce our testing time by directly asking for our lesson instead of fighting it. We continue to retake the test until we pass. We are never under trial without explicit permission by God. He allows our pruning seasons to prepare us for a greater yield. He wants us to learn something here to enable us to succeed at the next thing He has in mind. He may be preparing us to receive or acknowledge a blessing, or preparing us to be of use to someone else at the proper time.

Ask God to reveal His lesson plan. Be a good student. There is no need to stress or cram, because (Praise God) all our tests are open-book.

HANDLING A CHANGE OF PLANS

"I am the Lord's servant," Mary answered.
"May it be done to me as you have said."
LUKE 1:38

As women, our finest role model in the art of surrendered living is Mary. She was greeted by an angel, was probably terrified, and was told that she was to become an unwed mother and that her child would be none other than the Son of God.

She didn't react by screaming, fleeing, pouring a glass of wine, or calling a friend, "You are not going to believe this . . ."

No. She handled this amazing change of life's direction with courage and grace. Her surrender to God in the face of great change was absolute. Her unshakable faith and her resolute "Yes" changed the course of history.

How do we react when we are met with an unforeseen change in circumstance? How quickly can we adjust when plans change? When fear causes us to shrink back from living a surrendered life, we must think of Mary and remember that we, too, are handmaids of the Lord.

THE WIND ELUDES US

Better one handful with tranquillity than two handfuls with toil and chasing after the wind.

ECCLESIASTES 4:6

Our culture promotes chasing after the wind.

Messages come at us from all sides telling us "You don't have enough," "Here's a quick fix," or "Satisfaction guaranteed." We are conditioned to think that more is better, regardless of the method of acquisition or the deeper price extracted. We are profoundly exhausted from trying to do and be everything.

So much of our striving, posturing, and floundering is just chasing after the wind. We finally get what we thought we longed for, only to feel it elude our grasp and leave us hungrier than before. We have lost the significance of the words *enough* and *plenty*. All we know is *more*.

Prayer leads to gratitude, which breeds contentment. Think of all the ways God has given you enough; write them down if you need to. If we can recognize the futility of chasing wind, we can find the power to stop.

WHO DO YOU WORK FOR?

*Commit to the Lord whatever you do,
and your plans will succeed.*

PROVERBS 16:3

We fool ourselves by thinking we must do something great for God; that we must think of something incredible or promote ourselves for a better position of influence.

God wants us to beautify the ordinary and give meaning to the insignificant. He has placed us exactly where we are. He desires our submission rather than our might. We are called to make the best of whom and where we are *right now.*

Instead of daydreaming about potential big ideas and strategizing grand plans, start dedicating each day to the Lord. Whether you are home changing a diaper or out "changing the world," each task is equal. Commit your work to Him each day, and in doing so you will remain in the center of His will for your life. You will be blessed with purpose and peace beyond your understanding.

What matters is not what you are doing, but for whom.

HE IS FAITHFUL

God's gifts and his call are irrevocable.
ROMANS 11:29

Isn't it reassuring to know that God does not change His mind?

Aren't you grateful that He does not take back His invitations or His gifts? Isn't it wonderful that He doesn't get second thoughts about us?

When I consider the many ways I fall short, the opportunities I miss, and my willful disobedience, I am amazed that God persists with me. Despite all my weaknesses, He still loves me. He still blesses me. He still has mercy on me. He still finds use for me, turning my mistakes into His glory. He still has patience with me. He does not give up, even when I do.

For as unfaithful as I may be to Him, He is always faithful to me. The depth of His love for us is so humbling. Once He calls us, He continues to pursue us forever. Once He gifts us, He continues to favor us for a lifetime.

No matter what.

TIME TO LET GO

*"Leave your country and your people," God said,
"and go to the land I will show you."*
ACTS 7:3

We are a society of clingers. We cling to things that are best let go. How about tiny blobs of leftovers in Tupperware in the refrigerator—I mean, are you really going to eat that? Or old, free T-shirts from companies or events that we don't remember? Or piles of old magazines we intend to read one day when things slow down?

God wants us to rid ourselves of clutter and travel light in the direction of His leading. Some relationships move in that direction. Thank the Lord for them because they are treasures worth keeping. Other relationships drag us down, make us feel small or unworthy, and hinder our progress. We are called to let go at His command, as no earthly relationship is worth the sacrifice of not walking in the light to the land He plans to show us.

One Step at a Time

Come, follow me.
MATTHEW 4:19

Perhaps you know the joy of traveling with small children? At the top of a crowded escalator in the Denver airport, my twin three-year-old daughters froze with fear and refused to take my hands and step forward. Meanwhile, my five-year-old son and I were headed downstairs! When I realized the escalator beside us was also going down, I knew I had to get back up to them. Fighting my way through the crowd in the opposite direction, I finally got close to them and stretched out my arms, madly stair-stepping to maintain my position. Crying hysterically, at first they were too frightened to come to me. Then, realizing it was their best hope for safety, they stepped forward in trust and we made it safely down together.

When my heart stopped racing, it occurred to me that the Lord must feel as I did, always extending His hand and asking me to come with Him. Despite my fear, all I need to do is make the first step to show Him the intention of my direction. He sees my faltering, fledgling attempt at trust, and rewards me with the steadiness of His hand.

When God reaches out to you and calls your name, trust Him to guide you to safety.

THINGS LOOK DIFFERENT IN THE LIGHT

God is light; in him there is no darkness at all.
1 JOHN 1:5

When it comes to decision time or periods of uncertainty, there is a spiritual litmus test for every situation. The litmus test is whether or not our intended action will stand clearly in the light. God's way is light; His will does not mingle with the shadows.

If our words or choices would make us uncomfortable when exposed to the light, then we know that the path is not of God. When we make decisions in alignment with His will, we are immediately flooded with light. This light feels incomparably good; a pleasant rush of warmth and peace.

Try this litmus test and start purifying your motivations and straightening your path. When you are stuck, think first, *God is light.* Then walk in the direction of the light.

Whose Are You?

I know whom I have believed.

2 TIMOTHY 1:12

When it comes down to it, when you come to the cross-roads, the bitter end, where the rubber meets the road, when push comes to shove, what you believe is not sufficient.

You might believe in love, or that good triumphs over evil or that it will all work out in the end. Our world offers many ideas, options, and illusions as far as what to believe.

Sooner or later we get around to asking a better question. One with reach, depth, implication, and consequence.

Paul does not say to his protégé Timothy, "I know what I have believed." No, he makes a far more serious statement: "I know whom I have believed."

It's not what you believe, but whom. It isn't what you worship, it's whom. It's not in what you place your faith and trust, but in whom. You know who you are because you know whose you are.

Do you know Him?

YOU MUST CHOOSE

He who is not with me is against me,
and he who does not gather with me, scatters.

LUKE 11:23

If you want your clothes to be clean, do you run the load with tepid water? No, you put in detergent and bleach and crank up the heat! In the same sense, being spiritually luke-warm does not get the job done.

You do not walk closely with the Lord by default or accident. You must choose Him. It is a deliberate act of sacrificing your own gain for the glory of God. And it is not a choice made once. It is a choice made daily, moment by moment, to replace your will with His.

If you do not purposefully choose to be with Him, you choose against Him by default. When the winds of adversity tear through life, believers find shelter while the storm rages all around them. Those who do not believe have nowhere to go, no safe place to hide. The wind scatters them, easily dis-placing them and all the things they hold so dearly.

Choose your shelter deliberately and wisely. Be stead-fast and do not scatter.

LET HIM IN

The Lord does not look at the things man looks at.
Man looks at the outward appearance,
but the Lord looks at the heart.

1 SAMUEL 16:7

The image of the heart does not lie. The reflection of true self cannot be made lovely by false means. There is no surgery, makeup technique, or adornment that can successfully conceal a brittle heart or a spirit that is not at rest. A beautiful woman by outward standards quickly loses her beauty when her inner poison seeps through the cracks.

Ask the Lord to search your heart and show you what offends Him. Request His edifying light in the dank, dark corners of your ugly places. Ask Him to come and heal you *there*; show you what steps you need to take to reveal your true essence. When the heart is healed and healthy, a woman becomes radiant and transparent to the breathtaking beauty of the Lord.

Inward and outward luminosity cannot be achieved independently, but a simultaneous transformation is possible when God works on the heart.

Grant Him access.

TRUE HEALING OR SPIRITUAL SHORTCUT?

But thanks be to God! He gives us the victory through our Lord Jesus Christ.
1 CORINTHIANS 15:57

Would you rather have a perennial garden or a vase of cut flowers?

When Christ gives the victory, we are a garden blessed forever by seasons of bloom. He prunes and nourishes us. Each year we flourish with greater variety and depth as we grow into our beauty and inhabit our potential.

Victory through any other way is temporary at best.

Like cut flowers in a vase, what seems to be sufficient beauty for the moment is not alive. It is captured, limited, broken from its source . . . destined to brown, wither, and die. The same is true for us, if we choose methods of healing that are not of God. We will have a temporary beauty (perhaps merely a respite from pain, which seems like beauty) but nothing of lasting value. Nothing worth tending. When cut flowers die, we throw them away. When a garden starts to fade, we prune, weed, water, and replant.

When you have the choice to accept the bouquet or the seed, choose the option that will endure for eternity.

The only victory worth having is the one paid for in blood by the Savior of the world.

No Quick Fix

*Wait for the Lord; be strong and take heart
and wait for the Lord.*

PSALM 27:14

⁂

Our society values haste. Fast food, snap judgments, quick turnaround times, microwave ovens, the fast lane, shortcuts, quick-dry nail polish, and short engagements.

When we encounter a timeline we cannot control, we opt to rush things in our mind. We wish away the final months of pregnancy. We count down to the start of school. We are an era of "I'll be happy when . . ." people.

We must remind ourselves that timelines are not ours to control.

Do you want the quickest solution or the best possible outcome? Do you want to take the shortcut if the finest view lies a few more miles away, over the next hill? Do you want fast food or the delicacy of a fine meal? When your healing is at stake, take your time to make it thorough. Rushing into the next thing or person will not allow for a clean, deep heal. It will only postpone the real work that must be done; you will do it now or you will do it later.

Ask the Lord to teach you how to wait for His best with grace and hopeful expectancy.

CLEANING UP YOUR OWN YARD

When a man's ways are pleasing to the Lord,
he makes even his enemies live at peace with him.

PROVERBS 16:7

It takes practice to learn to pay no attention to what certain other people are doing. It takes training in the fine art of release not to heed whether someone else is happy, sad, successful, or floundering. To truly relinquish your interest and be totally absolved of seeking information regarding the affairs of others is a major step toward a life of freedom.

Before we can do anything else, we must focus our attention on what needs to be taken care of within our own area of responsibility. We often spend more time focusing on areas where others could change or improve, thus neglecting to sufficiently refine ourselves.

Our only area of effort and concern is to ensure our ways are pleasing to the Lord. Our own hearts, thoughts, and actions require more than enough energy in order to improve. When we focus on getting right with God, looking upward instead of outward toward others, He will take care of providing the peace in all our relationships.

WALK YOUR TALK

*Let us not love with words or tongue
but with actions and in truth.*

1 JOHN 3:18

Choices and behavior are more indicative of a changed heart than the words we speak.

It is one thing to say "I've changed" and quite another to actually prove it by your actions over time.

It is one thing to declare fidelity and another to love with strength, commitment, and integrity for a lifetime.

It is one thing to say "I love you," and another to love enough to allow someone to reap their own consequences.

It is one thing to tell a "harmless" white lie, and another to offer truth when the moment requires courage yet could incur risk or loss of relationship.

It is one thing to say "I'm sorry," and quite another to work from humility through repentance into grace.

Christ calls us to walk and not just talk. He wants our faith to shine like a lamp before others. He wants our words to reflect His Holy Spirit and our actions to be the fruit of a restored heart.

A Cause for Celebration

Be joyful in hope, patient in affliction, faithful in prayer.
ROMANS 12:12

We have our own foolish measures of protection against disappointment. We think if we don't react or get too excited about great possibilities, the letdown won't be as hard if things don't work out. The result is the limitation of our own joy and the reduction of our trust in God.

When we are constant in prayer and get to a deeper place of trust, we know that even if the rug is pulled out from under us, the Lord will grab us just before we fall on our faces. He will keep us steadfast if we stumble or suffer. This knowledge adds bravery to our hopefulness. We begin to try where we would normally hesitate. We begin to celebrate God's goodness and praise His works without knowing how it all will come together.

Have enough faith to give joy a chance. Celebrate the possibility.

TIME FOR REFLECTION

Where your treasure is, there your heart will be also.
MATTHEW 6:21

Tell me what you value.

A wise person said, "Show me your checkbook, and I'll tell you your values." Someone even wiser said, "Show me your calendar, and I'll tell you your values."

To me this Scripture applies to time, time as our treasure. Our days here are a numbered gift from God. How we decide to spend them is a reflection of our understanding of God's purpose for our lives. We are all given twenty-four hours in one day, yet why is it that some people stress and struggle while others manage to do and be many things well? Could it be that a greater reverence for the gift of time yields godly productivity?

Our expenditure of our time is where our intent and our actions collide. It is where we give life to our priorities. It's the way we carry our gratitude to God and carry the message of what we stand for to others.

Pray for clarity and consistency. Then look at your calendar and reflect upon your treasure.

ILLUMINATED STEPS

Jesus said, "I am the light of the world.
Whoever follows me will never walk in darkness,
but will have the light of life."

JOHN 8:12

I was playing a board game with my son Luke. Like many games, the spinner lands on a color and we move our game pieces ahead accordingly. A simple, orderly, relaxing process.

Not unlike following God.

When we request guidance and heed instruction, He gladly illuminates the path ahead. We don't have to flounder about in darkness, taking wrong turns and wasting precious time. His light shines before us, step-by-step . . . a simple, orderly, relaxing process.

To play correctly is not a matter of will or skill, but of submission . . . flow, not force. He calls us to have the faith of a child. Close your eyes and conjure a youthful spirit of playful obedience, expectation, and wonder.

NOTHING ON OUR OWN

Jesus said, . . . "I do nothing on my own."

JOHN 8:28

Jesus is our example of perfection. He was human like us, with all our weaknesses and temptations, yet He never faltered or wavered. He did not sin.

That seems to be a standard that is utterly impossible to strive for. By human understanding and standards, it is indeed impossible. But in this Scripture Jesus tells us His "secret." If He, the very Son of God, could do nothing apart from His Father, think how much more we need to rely on the Trinity.

We need the Holy Spirit to acquaint and align us with Jesus. We need Jesus to reconcile us to God. We need God to reconcile us to ourselves.

We can do nothing on our own.

LOVE NOTES

Whoever gives heed to instruction prospers,
and blessed is he who trusts in the Lord.

PROVERBS 16:20

❧

God's teaching comes in a variety of forms.

Sometimes His voice is a quiet whisper in our thoughts or in our dreams. Sometimes He reaches us through a message in a book or a lyric in a song. Sometimes He speaks literally through the mouth of a friend, mentor, stranger, or child. When Scripture leaps off the page and into our hearts with precision and relevance, it is because His word is alive. And sometimes no words are necessary at all when He sends personalized love notes in the language of our hearts. For me these love notes are sunrises, sunsets, unexpected hugs, pennies, and fireworks.

He is always speaking. We are occasionally listening. The key to heeding instruction and receiving His love notes is in maintaining an open heart as a clear channel to the truth. Attune your eyes, ears, and heart to the subtleties of His messages. Try to gain recognition of His gifts. Trust implicitly in His providence.

Allow Him to prosper and bless you.

THE AUTHOR OF YOUR STORY

As for God, his way is perfect.
PSALM 18:30

I have a habit that is annoying, disobedient, and truly the Achilles' heel in my spiritual walk. Maybe it's because I'm a writer that I think I can pen future chapters of my story. That somehow I know the plot twists and the character development needed to weave the richest tale—resulting in a happy, non-cliché ending. I imagine God has had many good laughs over me, watching me attempt to manipulate and massage my story to fit my outline.

He, of course, is the author of our faith, from start to finish, and He knows every page by heart. All the loose ends and fragments that seem to make no sense to me now, are all footnotes that fit perfectly into His grand design.

I must repent of my desire to write for myself, and hand my pen over to Him. I must repent of my tendency to flip ahead, skimming for clues and insight into what happens next and why. I want to live my life like the reading of a great novel, page by page savoring the descriptive details and soaking and relishing in the telling of it all.

WAKE UP TO A NEW DAY

This is the day the Lord has made;
let us rejoice and be glad in it.

PSALM 118:24

How many times have I heard the wise words that joy is independent of circumstances?

And yet, I admit to days when the alarm goes off and I feel the weight of the world has been stuffed into my duvet cover.

We have exactly two alternatives when we are burdened by unfavorable circumstances, of which divorce is no exception. We can sink into despair or we can rise up in praise and rejoice. We can thank God for everything good, and all the rest we don't comprehend yet. We can be thankful for things without particularly liking them at this moment. We can say, "Lord, You know this hurts. I don't understand what You are aiming for, but I will praise You in spite of my despair. I will thank You in advance for my future redemption and Your rebuilding of my life." We can go right on worshipping in the midst of chaos and confusion.

We can praise His mighty supernatural possibility or we can gridlock His blessing in discouragement.

Today is a new day. We have a fresh start. We can choose all over again.

BACK ON TRACK

[The Lord said,] "Return, faithless people;
I will cure you of backsliding."
JEREMIAH 3:22

There are times in our spiritual walk where we feel close to God and attuned to His will for us. We are working to be obedient and feel the warmth of His presence in our daily lives.

Other times, in our busyness, waywardness, or ingratitude, we stray.

We feel shame when we realize how disconnected and imbalanced we have become. We are all guilty of spiritual backsliding. We have good intentions, we know what we should be doing, and yet we slide.

Praise God that He is merciful and patient. He loves us so much that in spite of all our shortcomings, He simply asks us to return to Him. Our imperfection is smoothed by His grace. He alone can inspire and empower us to stay the course.

NOT JUST GOOD MANNERS

Give thanks in all circumstances,
for this is God's will for you in Christ Jesus.
1 THESSALONIANS 5:18

The operative word in this Scripture is the word—"in." Paul is not saying to be grateful for all good things—in fact, he is not saying to be grateful "for" anything. He is instructing us to live IN perpetual gratitude. This is a lifestyle choice, not a mood to cultivate or a proper response to blessing. Grateful people are free people, free to graciously accept what befalls us as a gift from His hands. There is power in thankfulness. The power is being able to rise above circumstance, knowing they are not permanent and they always have some redeeming purpose. When we thank God for all things, even the things that hurt, things we don't like or wouldn't choose, those things lose power over us. In praise we enter into the realm of Jesus.

In everything give thanks:
In spite of everything.
During everything.
Because of everything.
Through everything.
In the midst of everything.
Always, in everything . . .
Give thanks.

Receive What Is Yours Today

Afterward, as you know, when he wanted to inherit this blessing, he was rejected. He could bring about no change of mind, though he sought the blessing with tears.

HEBREWS 12:17

Right here, right now, in the midst of a very difficult year, you have a life-altering opportunity. You can reach for (and attain!) the ultimate blessing, available only through the inextricably intimate tie of discipline and mercy.

If you miss it, it will slip through your grasp, and the impact of what was lost will later grip you with gasping regret.

God seeks you, now.

He seeks to grant you wisdom, now. He longs to deeply bless you, now. Don't miss it.

There may be something else in store for you later, but perhaps not as bold or sublime. Later, when you realize what He meant for you, no amount of desire or tears will restore the golden moment inscribed with your name. Open your eyes when they are closed shut in fear. Open your heart before atrophy sets in. Open yourself completely to what is yours. Now.

THE SOURCE OF ALL LOVE

We love because he first loved us.

1 JOHN 4:19

✢

We don't love because we are generous of heart.
We don't love because we are obligated by relational chains.
We don't love because we are afraid not to comply.
We don't love because we are skilled at the game.
We don't love because we think this is all we deserve.
We don't love to stave off the void.
We don't love to feel validated.
We don't even love because we are healthy and whole.

No. We love for one reason only. *Because He first loved us.* Because we have been deeply and truly loved, we may love truly and deeply.

Not just once, but throughout a lifetime.

HEALING HANDS

*Then he put his hands on her, and immediately
she straightened up and praised God.*

LUKE 13:13

The weight of our burdens can literally cause us to bend
beneath them. We feel so heavy and hopeless that our entire
countenance takes on an air of oppression. We want to
hunch down, slink away, and go unnoticed.

The concept of laying hands on someone has always
borne the significance of healing . . . whether it is done by a
priest or an elder, a massage or physical therapist, or by a parent hovering over a sick child, touching their forehead. Many
ailing people in Jesus' time received the healing of His hands
directly upon them. We can pray for this blessing today.

While His hands are no longer flesh, they are pierced
and holy . . . spiritual hands of healing. Pray to the Lord to
use His mighty hands to lift your burden. Feel the
unfathomable comfort as He lightens of your load. As the
pressure eases, stand straight and tall and glorify God's
power with your gratitude.

STILL STANDING

Though it cost all you have, get understanding.
PROVERBS 4:7

Funny how it works . . . when everything you thought was most valuable is taken from you, the thing that truly is the most valuable is revealed. When you lose your marriage, your family, your money, your job, your status, your comfort zone, your health, your home, your friend, your reputation . . . anything you thought you could never do without; you realize with amazement that you are still standing.

That is when you finally realize that Jesus is the Rock. Sometimes we have to chip away at the earth to get to the rock.

Take solace that this understanding will prevent you from ever being so hurt or empty *ever again*. You are now equipped to face whatever comes your way. This is your workshop for faithful living.

Though it seems to have cost all you had, you finally understand that wisdom is priceless. Now you are ready to rebuild, this time with wisdom at the core.

MASTER ARTIST

I form the light and create darkness.

ISAIAH 45:7

༃

I am a painter. In the same sense that people sing in the shower or the car, I paint in private in a small studio above my garage. I don't paint to sell art or please critics. I paint to relieve a place in my soul that builds up and cannot be accessed through sleep, sweat, tears, words, or laughter.

If you asked me what I paint, I could not tell you. My art is the only aspect of my life that is untutored, undisciplined, and abstract. I put the intangibles of my emotion on canvas and enjoy the expression and interplay of color, texture, and light.

It comforts me to know that God is the master of my canvas. He controls the application and intensity of the color, and the contrast created by the shadows. We cannot critique an unfinished masterpiece. We must let Him complete His work in us.

ECLIPSE OF THE SON

The Holy Spirit will come upon you,
and the power of the Most High will overshadow you.

LUKE 1:35

I always considered myself a woman of vision. I like to picture good things happening, favorable circumstances working in alignment, and sweet surprises hidden along my way. I thought that the harder I tried, the more I would achieve. Until I hit some difficult times, I was one of those women who said without emotion or exception, "I can handle it," "I got it," or "I'm fine."

When I was at my weakest, and my ego was squashed, the Holy Spirit finally had some room to work in me. The power of the Most High literally had to overshadow me (actually, "eclipse me" is more accurate!) and my foolish sense of self-sufficiency. I struggled for a bit, valiantly trying to hang on to the "I'm fine" persona, but soon realized that I was far from doing fine. I didn't "have it."

It was very humbling to be overshadowed in this way, but humility quickly led to relief when I finally figured out that God never expected me to do it all, or to do anything well, all by myself.

THE INTIMACY OF TRUTH

Love and faithfulness meet together;
righteousness and peace kiss each other.

PSALM 85:10

❧

I love how Scripture can fluidly join concepts that appear to be oxymorons in the natural world.

How often do we avoid truth simply because we prefer to "be kind"? As if deceit is more acceptable? As if kindness and truth are contradictory or mutually exclusive? The Lord, by His Holy Spirit, enables each of us to speak the truth in love. Even if fear overtakes us and eloquence fails us, He will provide the courage and the vocabulary to take the leap of faith.

What is more intimate than a kiss? Do we see the inseparable link between righteousness and peace? Not if we are defining righteousness by our own standards or seeking it with our own hands. Again, only the Lord can bridge this gap of understanding . . . showing us that only by His love are the scales ultimately balanced.

What have you left unsaid that deserves utterance? Where does your healing require you to apply truth?

He Has Patience with Us

Those who are wayward in spirit will gain understanding;
those who complain will accept instruction.

ISAIAH 29:24

❧

I am not sure you could pack more mercy or more hope into one single sentence.

I am a great source of frustration to myself. I fall short of God's mark when I know better. I disappoint Him, and myself, on a regular basis. If my walk with the Lord is on forest trails, I have purposefully bent branches enough times to know how often I have to repeat lessons and take the path again.

Jesus is the most patient teacher. He tenderly and carefully explains to me each time what His expectations are and why He believes I can do better. He thoughtfully reflects my criticism of others into a mirror and reveals the areas in need of improvement within my own heart.

This Scripture reassures me that for all the times I mess up, I am not doomed. I'm not saying His rebukes feel good, but it is obvious to me by His firm yet gentle guidance that He desires the best for me. He intends to heal, not hurt me.

Words Become Reality

He who guards his lips guards his life.

PROVERBS 13:3

In the same way that your thoughts become your actions and your actions define your character, your words have the power to alter your future. Like an actress rehearses her lines to become her new persona, the words you rehearse over and over become the role you play. Your dialogue becomes your script, and your script becomes the story of your life.

When you speak blessings, you are automatically blessed. When you say things that glorify God and the great future He has in store for you, your praises turn into your positive reality. When you are deliberate and wise in choosing your speech, you honor the Lord with your mouth. If you aren't sure, your hesitation could be a trigger from the Holy Spirit to choose silence instead of making a verbal misstep.

Monitor your thoughts and take them captive before they become words. Guard your gift of proclamation by speaking good things, healing things, and give the truth a voice in you.

STEP OUT IN GRATITUDE

Give thanks to the Lord.

PSALM 105:1

Thank You, Lord, for carrying me through this day.

Thank You, Lord, for strengthening me beyond my circumstances today.

I praise You, Lord, for Your healing hands surrounding my heart.

Thank You, Lord, for quieting my anxious thoughts.

I praise You, Lord, that You work all things together for my good.

Thank You, Lord, for protecting the innocence of my children.

I praise You, Lord, that You never allow me to take a single step without Your guidance.

Thank You, Lord, that You are Lord over all my relationships.

Thank You, Lord, for being Lord over every area of my life.

One morning during my quiet time, I changed my whiny petitions into confident statements of gratitude. Although at the time my situation felt overwhelming, I decided to be hopeful and thankful instead of discouraged and fearful. It was a step of faith that got me going in the right direction. My prayer life was permanently altered that day as I learned the power of praise.

Amen!

Hungry in Spirit

Lord, when did we see you hungry and feed you, or thirsty and give you something to drink?

MATTHEW 25:37

In one sense this verse reminds me of homeless people and how important it is to view the world and its inhabitants with fresh eyes of compassion. I literally think of seeing the face of God in the downtrodden and hungry and giving them food or drink.

This is an easy and direct application. But take it to another level and ask yourself if you see the face of God in those who are aching, lonely, empty, or hopeless . . . those with emotional and spiritual malnourishment. Perhaps they seem "normal" or "okay" to the untrained, busy eye. But if you take the time to see through the facade to their spirits—are you brave enough to see their pain?

Are you bold enough to call attention to their burden by offering to shoulder it with them for a while? Are you filled enough to offer your abundance to the spiritually starved?

Lord, help me to see the need You place in my path today. Take me outside myself as I help someone else.

How, Lord?

Blessed is the man who perseveres under trial, because when he has stood the test, he will receive the crown of life that God has promised to those who love him.

JAMES 1:12

Scottish minister Oswald Chambers said that "unless we can look the darkest, blackest fact full in the face without damaging God's character, we do not yet know Him."

We may never understand the "Whys?" of life on this side of heaven, but trust does not answer "Why?" questions; it answers "How?" questions.

How am I going to get through this?
How will I sleep tonight?
How will I take care of my children?
How will I pay the bills?
How will I ever love again?
Answer: trust.

In answering these "How" questions, we are not looking for an answer, but for the author of the answer. Jesus answers all of these questions by offering the sufficiency of Himself. Trust is the only way to persevere under trial. It is the only way to stand the test. Trust is the only way to receive the crown of life that God has promised to those who love Him.

WE DON'T KNOW

Judge nothing before the appointed time;
wait till the Lord comes.

1 CORINTHIANS 4:5

Paige's mother, Suzy, usually responds to any new piece of information with the simple statement "We don't know."

Such and such happened to so-and-so. Isn't that awful?

We don't know.

Can you believe the news about so-and-so? Isn't that wonderful!

We don't know.

It may sound simplistic or trite, but the truth in this short, evasive sentence is profound. Truly, we don't know. Who are we to judge blessing or misfortune? Our perception is puny and our vision clouded by spiritual cataracts. I perceived my divorce as my ultimate misfortune. I thought I was cursed or utterly disposable, no one worth fighting for. Yet He fought for me. Through my greatest pain, the Lord gave me the gift of faith and a fresh start. He returned me to myself, through the path of Himself.

When something befalls you, good or bad, think of Suzy and stay spiritually neutral.

After all, *we don't know.*

OPEN TO DESIRE

No discipline seems pleasant at the time, but painful.
Later on, however, it produces a harvest of righteousness
and peace for those who have been trained by it.

HEBREWS 12:11

I recently went to a retreat based on the book *Captivating* by John and Stasi Eldredge. Stasi eloquently explains that in every trial we are called to remain "open to living with desire."

In the face of great loss or challenge, we must choose to open to God, to the experience and the lessons, and be deliberate about not shutting down. There was a period of time where I felt safer with my heart in lockdown. I figured if no one could reach my heart, no one could hurt it again. This is an emotional cop-out, and a spiritual error of grave consequence. This retreat was a wake-up call to me, telling me it was insufficient to hide my heart away, that avoiding pain was not a way to live a life for God.

No, it's not pleasant to be in pain. But it's even more unpleasant to miss an important opportunity to be trained by God, especially when the lesson comes again and again until we get it right. Open your heart to receive the training you need.

This time of great effort will yield a substantial and satisfying harvest.

Peace in the Present Moment

If they obey and serve him, they will spend the
rest of . . . their years in contentment.

JOB 36:11

✑

If I knew tomorrow was the last day of my life, I would get up early. I would make coffee and have my prayer time before the kids woke up. I would praise God for all the days He gave me. I would snuggle my children and make pancakes for breakfast in the midst of noise and chaos in my kitchen. I would pack lunches, braid hair, find shoes, brush teeth, and hand out backpacks. I'd probably drive to school in my pajamas. I'd pray a blessing over my children in the car and kiss everyone. After I was alone, I'd go running. I'd feel my lungs and legs burn and notice the way the sunlight filters through the trees along Town Lake. I would try to meet a girlfriend for coffee. I would call my parents and my brother to say, "Hi, how are you? I love you."

In other words, on my final day, I would do the same exact things I do every day. I would live the life I am living right now. If I had to choose, I'd choose what I have.

What does this say about where my level of gratitude should be? Perhaps I should pursue my abundance in this moment and cease focusing on the holes. Praise for all that is, not pity what is not.

Thank You, God, for right now.

SEEK VALIDATION FROM ONE SOURCE

*You will keep in perfect peace him whose
mind is steadfast, because he trusts in you.*

ISAIAH 26:3

✸

There are people in my life I will never be able to please or impress. Folks who will never say, "Good job," "Impressive work," or "Congratulations." In fact, their words are often the voice of the enemy, speaking aloud my deepest regrets, fears, inadequacies, and doubts about myself.

If I take their opinion into account, I will feel like a failure every time. I have allowed my peace to be stolen far too many times, and it's time to change.

What a sweet release to remember that my purpose is not to please anyone but God alone. It is not only discouraging to elevate the opinion of others, but it is actually a sin—idolatry. Modern-day idolatry is putting something or someone ahead of God. He is the one source of true validation. His is the only definition of our identity that matters.

God states my purposes and gives me perfect peace when I keep my eyes focused on Him and do not look elsewhere.

Undercover Agents

So we fix our eyes not on what is seen,
but on what is unseen. For what is seen
is temporary, but what is unseen is eternal.

2 CORINTHIANS 4:18

As I write this I am in my stylist's chair at the salon. It appears that Suzanne's job is to be a hairstylist; that is what is seen. Beyond that, each of us has a purpose and a role that is not seen . . . but is vastly more significant.

Suzanne ministers to her clients, sharing the message of the gospel while she cuts, highlights, and blow-dries hair. She uses unseen opportunities to excel at her "real job." We are all undercover agents in this way; we do our appointed work for the Lord under the guise of other careers and roles in this life. I like to think of this as the ministry of the mundane, and at its core is the essence of how we treat people. The gospel message is a bold one. Our job is not to water the message down to make it more appealing but to water ourselves down (our ego, pride, self-righteousness) so that the message is seen more clearly in the way we live our lives. Big things can happen in small ways when our warm and nonjudgmental natures attract people to the Lord.

Don't let opportunities pass you by.

IDENTITY IN CHRIST

*The Lord your God has chosen you out of
all the peoples on the face of the earth to
be his people, his treasured possession.*

DEUTERONOMY 7:6

Yep. You.

You are a treasured possession of the Father of the universe. You have been selected, set aside, called upon, and gold-starred. You, out of all the people on the face of the earth, are known and preferred.

Do you live in the light of the knowledge of your identity? Do you know who you are in God's eyes? Is your confidence based on this value? Are your expectations aligned with your divine destiny? Do you make choices based on a reasonable standard of what you deserve? Can you calmly say, "No, thank you," and walk away from someone or something that is beneath God's hope for you?

Or are you, just maybe, playing small?

Playing small and aiming low serves no one. It is not a sign of humility to belittle yourself and your life—it is humility to know who you are in relation to God.

ROCK-SOLID

He is the Rock, his works are perfect,
and all his ways are just.
DEUTERONOMY 32:4

Look around in nature these days and we see earthquakes, tsunamis, hurricanes, floods, erosion, and fires. There is no place safe to stand in the natural world that cannot be shaken, washed away, blown away, burned, or turned to dust. You no doubt felt that way when your marriage was dissolved. But take courage. There is a spiritual safe house that remains untouched by the casualties of this life. There is a relationship that will not fail you, or permit you to continue to fail yourself. There is a Rock that offers a foundation that cannot crack or erode.

Our Lord is the only Rock upon which you can rebuild your life.

He is the only sure place to stand in these turbulent times. Regardless of trial and circumstance, and our perception or emotion relative to where we are, we know by faith that God is perfect and just. His dealings with us are always what we need, if not always what we want.

We all long for protection and stability.

We all long for the Rock.

SWEET REDEMPTION

Thus says the Lord, your Redeemer, the Holy One of Israel, "I am the Lord your God, who teaches you to profit, who leads you in the way you should go."

ISAIAH 48:17

I love Jesus' title of *Redeemer*.

He can redeem any person, any life, and any circumstance. Nothing is too much, too messy, too far gone, or too hard for Him. He works all things together for good for those who love Him.

He tells us that we belong to Him; just as He belongs to us. He teaches us to profit—in all ways. We profit financially by using the gifts He gives us. We profit mentally by gaining wisdom through experience and emotionally by learning to make good choices in love. We profit physically by living in a state of balance and health. We profit spiritually by focusing on eternity instead of present pain. He will lead us when we hand the reins of our lives over to Him.

We must give up control and allow Him to redeem us, bless us, prosper us, and guide us.

STEP OUTSIDE

A generous man will prosper; he who
refreshes others will himself be refreshed.

PROVERBS 11:25

When I'm having a rough or moody day and am tempted to feel sorry for myself, I try to give the Lord access to turn things around. Of course Jesus has the ability and the authority to turn things around, but He prefers to come where He's invited.

Put this Scripture promise to the test. The next time you feel like hosting a pity party for yourself, take alternative steps and reach out to someone else instead. Go out of your way to listen, bless, or refresh. When you help to alleviate the pain or stress of another, you will miraculously find your own load lightened considerably.

God refreshes those who refresh others.

Do something for someone else when you feel that you don't have much to offer. You might be surprised at the bountiful way your own storehouse is replenished.

Take steps to step outside yourself today.

A DIVINE REPLANTING

The Lord will guide you always;
he will satisfy your needs in a sun-scorched land.

ISAIAH 58:11

The Lord knows your inner landscape, no matter the painstaking efforts you make to beautify the outside. He knows your topography, your terrain, the expected yield of your personal harvest. He knows where you are, and where you need to be, and He's the only one who can get you back on track.

He knows the scorched places of your unmet desire.

Don't be afraid or ashamed to invite Him into your wasteland. He wants to replant and irrigate, knowing the richness of land hidden under ruins. When He works your field, nothing is wasted . . . not time, not relationships, not pain, not any experience. He uses everything. The decomposition of one life can fertilize the next.

The Lord will guide you. He will direct you and teach you how to fortify yourself. He might encourage you to wait a season before replanting. Or He may surprise you with unexpected blooms.

Trust Him to minister to you in your desolate places.

HONOR HIM BY LOVING WELL

[God] will not forget your work and the love you have
shown him as you have helped his people.

HEBREWS 6:10

You might be tired. You may be weary of plugging along the right path. You may see no apparent fruit in your routine. It's hard on the ego when effort seems to go unnoticed.

But don't give up.

Don't give in.

God sees what other people don't see. He is more interested in your "why" and "how" than your "what." He sees your heart, your intent, and your perseverance. As you do your work and love those around you, you honor God in an unforgettable fashion. You praise God by your quiet efforts. Mother Teresa said, "We can do no great things, only small things with great love."

When your energy wanes and you long to see some sign of His providence—it is here your faith is promoted to a new level. Ask the Lord to refresh you, and He will graciously grant you the endurance you desire.

GUIDANCE GIVEN FREELY

Call to me and I will answer you and tell you
great and unsearchable things you do not know.
JEREMIAH 33:3

Did you know that you can ask God for wisdom, discernment, intuition, guidance, and supernatural understanding?

It seems pretty bold, I know, but we have been invited to ask. God sees everything. He has the overhead view of the maze of our lives and knows every turn, pitfall, and dead end. We stumble along with a limited view that extends only to the next curve in our path.

We can't ask for guidance only when we get ourselves into a fix. We must be more disciplined to ask for guidance daily. Perhaps we can even avoid some pitfalls and dead ends.

Before you plant your feet on the floor next to your bed in the morning, ask God to direct your steps. Forget the missteps of yesterday and the fear of the unknown tomorrow, and ask God to guide you today.

FOLLOWING SIGNS

Set up road signs; put up guideposts.
Take note of the highway, the road that you take.
JEREMIAH 31:21

It's dangerously easy to veer off track. We might exit our route to take a brief scenic side street and suddenly find ourselves utterly lost and delayed.

I take this Scripture literally and place visual signs in various places. There are crosses around my house that are purposeful triggers to pray for certain people and things. There are Scriptures on sticky notes in random places—on my car visor to remind me to bless my children before they leave and to continuously thank God for our safety and protection. There's another on my bathroom cabinet to remind me that true beauty is not found by looking in the mirror.

More are stuck in my kitchen prompting me to praise God for His provision and to pray to God for patience during the hectic hour before dinner. I know I need these road signs; I know I am lost without constantly referring back to my directions.

COMFORT SOURCE

May [the Lord's] unfailing love be my comfort.
PSALM 119:76

My twin daughters carry blankets. Grace calls hers "blankie," and Bella calls hers "softie." In the shuffle between Mom's house and Dad's house, these are the two items that cannot be forgotten or misplaced. We have spent hours over their relatively short life spans hunting around for these blankets, or retrieving them from other places.

Sometimes these blankets frustrate me. Do we *really* have to drive back there and look for that?

Yes, we do.

Because "blankie" and "softie" are not just cloth, they are comfort. They represent security, warmth, consistency, and love. Who am I to deem them unnecessary or childish? Just because I am thirty years older does not mean that my desire for comfort is any different or any less.

Praise God that my comfort is always with me. It cannot be misplaced or forgotten. I always know right where it is. The Lord's unfailing love is exactly where it should be when I need it—*right here.*

GRACE IN WEAKNESS

*Let us then approach the throne of grace with
confidence, so that we may receive mercy and
find grace to help us in our time of need.*

HEBREWS 4:16

It's amazing to think about approaching God's throne with
confidence in a time of need. In my time(s) of need I feel
more comfortable slumping on the sofa surrounded by
balled-up Kleenexes.

When we are at our worst is precisely when we need to
seek out the best.

We need to get off the sofa, dust ourselves off, take a
deep breath, and approach our heavenly Father. We can call
on the confidence of Christ to compensate for our unworthiness and weakness. When it comes to God, our confidence
is based in weakness because it is in our weakness that His
power and grace are revealed. When we finally get in touch
with our own need is when He can begin to fill it. When we
offer our sorrow to Him, He can manifest His promise to
turn it into joy. When we offer our anxiety and fearfulness,
He can show us the depth of His peace in deeper contrast.

Remember, He does not see us the way we see ourselves; He sees us the way we are meant to be.

TOO SOON TO TELL

Look, you scoffers . . . for I am going to do something in your days that you would never believe, even if someone told you.

ACTS 13:41

What if someone told you that everything happening to you now was like a bad dream, and soon enough you would wake up in a better place? What if the same someone also told you that all true reality was behind the scenes and God was at work, right at this very minute, preparing something so wonderful for you that it was impossible for you to conceive it or believe it?

What if your wildest dreams, your most unfathomable series of impossibly perfect blessings, were rejected as not good enough for you?

What if you heard, "Hold tight. Be patient with me. I've got everything under control, and I can't wait to surprise you"?

Well, guess what, fellow scoffer? Someone is telling you this! Not just once, but over and over again. The Creator of the universe is paging you over the loudspeaker, and He wants you to meet Him at the information booth.

He has a message for you:

I am going to do something in your days that you would never believe, even if someone told you.

SHIFT IN PERSPECTIVE

I will rescue you on that day, declares the Lord; you will not be handed over to those you fear. I will save you; you will not fall by the sword but will escape with your life, because you trust in me, declares the Lord.

JEREMIAH 39:17–18

❧

Are you holding on tightly with your eyes closed? Are you clinging to something that is slipping out of your hands? Are you fighting your own release? Are you screaming and clawing, unaware that the door has been unhinged and removed?

What does the phrase *"[you] will escape with your life"* mean to you?

Does that sound like a victim? Does that sound like a persecuted and scorned woman? No way, girl. That sounds like a victor to me. A free woman. A hall pass. A get-out-of-jail-free card. A second chance. A do-over.

It's the same exact scenario, with a perspective shift. Try it. Sometimes all it takes is a tiny step in a different direction to change our perspective. For example, did someone leave you or are you now free? Did someone discard you or are you recently liberated to love elsewhere? Are you a failure because your marriage did not work out or are you trying to work hard because your marriage failed?

This is your life, still and always. Make it your best life. He's holding the door for you.

Go.

Preparation of the Heart

Prepare the way for the Lord, make straight paths for him. Every valley shall be filled in, every mountain and hill made low. The crooked roads shall become straight, the rough ways smooth. And all mankind will see God's salvation.

LUKE 3:4–6

As John the Baptist prepared the world for Christ, we too are called to prepare our hearts for Him.

Some of this preparation comes via the hand of circumstance. Some experiences are so leveling that we have no mountains anymore. Other more refined and subtle methods of preparation come from the whispers of the Holy Spirit. The rough areas within us will be smoothed and refined, the brush and debris will be moved aside to clear the path for the Lord.

Ask God to help you prepare your heart for His service. Ask Him to purify and cleanse your thoughts, attitudes, and motives. He will direct your path, leading you on the most direct and scenic routes to get you where you are supposed to be—at the right place at the right time for the meeting of a lifetime.

God wants to glorify His power and provision through you. Let Him.

IT IS ALREADY DONE

I thank and praise you, O God of my fathers:
you have given me wisdom and power,
you have made known to me what we asked of you,
you have made known to us the dream of the king.

DANIEL 2:23

Certainly wisdom and power would remarkably alter our present circumstances. Wisdom would allow us to think our way out and power would see that we were not stopped along the way. God is the embodiment of wisdom and power, and what's more, He wants to share those traits with His children.

When you feel short in these areas, the best course of action is worship. Praise God for granting what you are lacking, praise Him in advance for remedying the situation and watch with wonder at what happens next. When I am afraid, I praise God for giving me great courage. When I'm utterly at a loss for what to say or do, instead of despairing, I thank God for directing my steps. Praise unlocks Power. Faith is thanking God for something He has not even done yet, because you know without a doubt that He will act on your behalf.

It can be as simple as changing the tense of the verb in your prayers. It isn't audacity; it's trust. Thank God for what He has "already done," and He will reward your faith.

REFLECTING ON SIN

*What benefit did you reap at that time
from the things you are now ashamed of?*
ROMANS 6:21

It is nearly impossible to see the snare of sin when we are in the grip of it. At the very best we can feel its symptoms (a call for deception, anxiety, regret, etc.) and recall lessons learned in our past.

When the pulse of sin is racing within us, it is so temporarily attractive that we block out the potential consequences. The law of sowing and reaping is inalterable.

Paul challenges us to look back into previous sin. And if this weren't painful enough, he then asks us to consider what benefits resulted from our behavior. Chances are— none. Sin hurts us, and it hurts those we love. By keeping our memories fresh of where we have fallen short in the past, we will guard the humility that comes from knowing how easily we can fall again.

We must cling to God.

No Limits

With man this is impossible,
but with God all things are possible.
MATTHEW 19:26

Imagine the vista of life through eyes of understanding.
Imagine the softness of a heart enriched by forgiveness and
mercy.
Imagine the satisfaction of ceasing to expect.
Imagine the relief of not pretending to have all the answers.
Imagine relearning about love from the author of love Himself.
Imagine being humble enough to ask for help when you need
it.
Imagine the ease of knowing you are enough.
Imagine the rest of perfect union with the lover and keeper of
your soul.

These are not lofty ideals to aspire to; these notions cannot be achieved through self-discipline or grueling effort. We cannot scramble to collect these graces; they are handed out slowly as we open ourselves to new levels of understanding and learn to receive. These are gifts no one has enough money to pay for. These are fruits of a life of faith, the pleasant grace of surrender, and the comforts of coming home.

MAKE ROOM FOR A VIEW

I was not disobedient to the vision from heaven.

ACTS 26: 19

We were created to require hope. This is why all roads eventually lead to God. Without a vision for our lives, we are lost souls wandering without purpose or fulfillment.

A vision is not the same as a plan. I am a list person, so I can make notes, resolutions, and list goals and objectives with ease. But this carries us only to the periphery of our own perceived ability and identity—nowhere close to our own potential, even further yet from God's inspired will for our lives.

A vision forces us to "see" something; it's very different from a list. It requires openness and trust to begin to see ourselves as God sees us . . . to remove our self-imposed barriers and merge our meagerness into the stream of God's power, where all things are possible.

Ask the Lord to give you vision.

YOU HAVE WHAT YOU NEED

As for you, the anointing you received from him remains in you, and you do not need anyone to teach you.

1 JOHN 2:27

When a big decision or crisis moment presents itself, do you feel the need to take an opinion poll?

It is one thing after prayer to seek godly counsel or additional prayer support from trusted accountability partners. It is quite another to recount your situation or current quandary countless times looking for dramatic validation or a nugget of inspiration. In doing so, we waste precious time and energy that could be used in more powerful ways. It is a natural desire, but one that must be given up.

When you were anointed with the Holy Spirit, it was your first installment of your heavenly plan. You were given a pathway to wisdom. When life gets crazy or confusing, your job is to get quiet. Ask for revelation and wait patiently. Your relationship with the Lord is sufficient unto itself. You have no real need to go elsewhere.

You will receive the guidance that you have been promised.

A Complete Overhaul

He who was seated on the throne said,
"I am making everything new!"
REVELATION 21:5

All things. Not just some things. Everything.

Everything about your life can and will be renewed. God begins with the renovation of your heart and works outward, touching every aspect of your life.

He will make you brand-new. He will replenish all your relationships. He will cast your circumstances in a new light. He will renew your energy to ensure you have enough courage and endurance. He will reinvigorate your faith. He will give you clear eyes to see His majesty in everything and everyone. He will give you fresh understanding and an awakening of appreciation.

A small smile will spread into a full-blown grin as you watch Him work His magic on you. He fits it all together one puzzle piece at a time, giving you a whole new picture.

A DEFEATED ENEMY

*Though they plot evil against you and
devise wicked schemes, they cannot succeed.*

PSALM 21:11

∾

Appearances can be very deceiving. The smiling family in the restaurant may be hiding unspeakable pain. The prominent leader in the community might be abusive at home. A charming smile can be laced with ice.

So it is with times of trial and disappointment. The enemy may be rejoicing in our pain and present defeat, thinking we will finally turn away from God.

The very season we currently groan over and despise, may just be the divine link in a chain of blessings too rich and too complex to imagine.

God can create harmony, in fact masterful symphony, out of the most discordant instruments. He can cajole blinding beauty out of the mundane. He can gift-wrap life's most precious surprises in the bleakest of coverings. The one who means evil against you is a puppet subject to the hand of the Master of the universe.

He can take the evil and repurpose it for good. He has not forgotten you.

RAISE YOUR HAND

Then I heard the voice of the Lord saying,
"Whom shall I send? And who will go for us?"
And I said, "Here am I. Send me!"

ISAIAH 6:8

The point here is to be ready.

Our lives are our classrooms, our trials are our workshops. The Lord sends us teachers and prepares our exams. We are in a constant state of preparation, never knowing what will be expected of us or when He will deem us ready.

The Lord will ensure our education and experience, but we must be willing and ready. We must be bold enough to raise our hands and say, "Here I am. Send me!"

It is not a matter of being good enough, strong enough, or smart enough. It's about eventually reaching a point where we have sufficiently faded into the background of ourselves, allowing people to see God first. Your pain has purpose. You are gaining wisdom, compassion, humility, and grace. Soon you will be called upon to help someone else, perhaps someone following in your footsteps along this difficult path. Be ready.

The Promise of His Presence

For the Lord your God is a merciful God;
he will not abandon or destroy you.
DEUTERONOMY 4:31

Stick this promise directly in the face of abandonment. Watch that spirit shrivel up and slink away.

Abandonment is, unfortunately, a great fear for many women. It poisons relationships and often keeps women prisoners in unhealthy situations. Perhaps you have been abandoned by your husband . . . physically and emotionally. Perhaps this abandonment stems from similar experiences in your childhood. The greatest loss in the wake of abandonment is the inability to trust. And like any great loss, the Lord can redeem it. The greater the loss, the greater the testimony to God's greatness.

This Scripture is the spiritual antidote to your fear and lack of trust.

We do not have to fear the departure of anyone if we know that God will never leave us. Yes, we may have temporary feelings of loneliness, but if He is with us we have nothing to fear. And He promises His presence always, to the end of the age.

CUPCAKES

For I am the Lord, your God, who takes hold of your right hand and says to you, Do not fear; I will help you.

ISAIAH 41:13

I will never forget the sad image of myself standing in my kitchen, trying to frost cupcakes for Luke's class. I was trying so hard to be normal, to go on smoothly with the regular duties of life. But suddenly it all seemed too much for me. I sat down and cried, still holding my frosting-covered spatula, shaking and broken.

Right then, my friend Paige let herself in and entered my kitchen, somehow (thank You, God) knowing I needed her. She literally picked me up off the floor and helped me finish my frosting. She was the voice of God for me that day: "Fear not, I will help you."

I still smile, and probably always will, every time I frost a cake. It always reminds me of how much God loves me, and how sweet life can be, even in the midst of pain.

IN HIS ARMS

His left hand is under my head,
and his right arm embraces me.

SONG OF SONGS 2:6

Could there be a more tender depiction of compassion and comfort? Imagine this scene between you and the Lord: you, in all your pain and brokenness, are held in His arms. His left hand cradles your feverish head, and His right arm embraces you in all your frailty. In this moment you find solace in the healing arms of the Son of God.

This intimacy is real. This compassion is spiritually tangible. This is the place you find yourself when the bottom falls out of your life and you plummet through the abyss, landing with a thud. Suddenly there He is. When you awake, you find yourself in His arms, marveling at the bizarre combination of bad and good fortune. Take time to revel in His loving embrace. Be comfortable and secure in a love that abides.

WALKING IN GOOD COMPANY

Do not be yoked together with unbelievers.
2 CORINTHIANS 6:14

Maybe this summed up your marriage, or maybe it didn't.

Either way, you have a precious opportunity to create a new life now. You can choose openly to place Christ at the center of your household, and the center of your family. You can choose to date only believers. You can deliberately surround yourself with godly friends. Every single thing that has fallen away can be replaced with something that endures. You can choose to do it all differently now. You can live a life in the light.

The primary relationships in your life need to elevate you, encourage your faith, instruct you, inspire you, comfort you, and challenge you. If you have committed to walk with Christ, you need to take steps to align yourself with like-minded people.

Choose to be with those who share your values, your priorities, your faith, and ultimately your eternal destiny.

SPEAK UP!

Our help is in the name of the Lord.

PSALM 124:8

Sometimes we feel so defeated that we forget we have options! We can choose victory over defeat by claiming God's promises in the name of Jesus.

Speaking Jesus' name out loud wields incredible power. His is the name at which all the world will bend their knees. You alone can do precious little, but with His name you can create options, find safety, generate power, and summon amazing courage in the face of despair. Prayers in the silence of the mind are sufficient for some occasions, but in treacherous times we must speak out loud without timidity.

If you find yourself in a moment of danger or confusion, call on the Lord. When you see no possible solution or escape, speak your plea out loud to the only one who could possibly do anything for you.

Our help comes from one source, one direction.

Call on Him out loud with confident faith.

FIRST PLACE

You shall not make for yourself an idol.
EXODUS 20:4

❧

God says flat out that He is a jealous God.

The Creator and Redeemer of all does not take kindly to anything less than first place.

An idol can be anything that infringes on or takes the place of God in our lives . . . a person, money, sex, power, food, alcohol, career, exercise, children, or service.

Look closely at your daily calendar and review the previous month. Where do you spend your time and attention, or your money? Is there anything or anyone that is taking an improper percentage of your time? Are you too busy to pray? Is your life too noisy to find quiet? Are you too frenetic to find stillness? Do you care to impress anyone more than you want to impress God?

Carefully search out the roadblocks between you and God. Ask the Lord to shed His light on your modern-day idolatry and give you the power to cast it down.

Teachable Moments

[Jesus said,] "You call me 'Teacher' and 'Lord,'
and rightly so, for that is what I am."

JOHN 13:13

Jesus has many titles.

Lately I have meditated more on His titles of Healer and Redeemer. Perhaps I need to spend more time thinking of Him as my Teacher.

Through the course of becoming single again, I experienced many unexpected events and disappointing surprises. When I am blindsided by something, I want my first thought to be, *Okay, Lord, I know You are involved here someplace. I know You haven't left me. Tell me, Teacher, what is it You want me to learn here?* I have not once asked for my lesson where I have not gotten a response. Like any great teacher, He delights in instruction and revels in the success of His students.

Imagine how that might please the Lord! Instead of becoming angry or inconsolable, we should be eager students looking for clues to unlocking the mystery of knowledge and spiritual wisdom. I long to be one of God's favorite pupils.

Help me, Lord, not to complain about my lessons.

A GIVING SOUL

A generous man will prosper;
he who refreshes others will himself be refreshed.
PROVERBS 11:25

The classic dieter's dilemma: You want to lose weight so you eat less. This sends a message to your body that says, "Uh-oh, prepare for the worst! Downshift into starvation mode!" So your metabolism plummets, along with your energy level and any hope for success. Your body greedily clutches calories, and no weight comes off. Wiser, healthier people know that if you want to lose weight, you need to do the opposite—eat well.

Spiritually healthy people know that if you want to live well, you have to give well.

In times of emotional trauma, we can clutch our gifts greedily to our chests, downshift into spiritual starvation, and turn inward. Like the poor, uneducated dieter, the scale never shifts! Only by opposing our nature and giving when we feel poor or helping when we feel helpless can we receive what we need.

LOVE MULTIPLIES

One man gives freely, yet gains even more;
another withholds unduly, but comes to poverty.

PROVERBS 11:24

This Scripture can be literally applied to material generosity; we know that if we give freely, we will be blessed.

But let's absorb this verse on a deeper level and think in terms of emotional and spiritual benevolence. When I was pregnant with my daughters I would lament to my mother about the fear of shortchanging my son when his sisters were born. Like somehow there would not be enough of me to go around. My mom smiled and reminded me that love multiplies; it does not divide.

If we give freely from the reservoirs of our true selves, we will be more than replenished; we will overflow. Give love when you feel empty. Forgive when you feel unable. Minister when you are tired. Embrace when resentment swells. Share spiritual gifts you aren't sure you possess. These things come from the Lord and are not yours to withhold. Give and grow.

TALK IS CHEAP

If I testify about myself, my testimony is not valid.
JOHN 5:31

Right here we have a fine lesson in humility, spoken by the Son of God.

We can apply it to our meager selves as well. We have no need to jockey for a better position, no need to make sure our good deeds and noble intentions are known. It is not necessary to toot our own horns; in fact, it is downright repelling. We don't need to pretend we can fight our battles . . . we look ridiculous all suited up for combat.

When we are hurting and our egos our bruised, it is tempting to try to ascertain our value with our words. But as Jesus says, our own testimony is invalid! We cancel ourselves out! Aim for silent action, quiet courage, soft and deliberate progress. Steady work, not flash, is the harbinger for true change.

We don't even have to use words to testify about what God has done. By being in the presence of a spirit-filled, humble person, everyone around is aware. Everyone wants to know more. Everyone wants a piece of that peace.

SEE YOURSELF CLEARLY

*When pride comes, then comes disgrace,
but with humility comes wisdom.*

PROVERBS 11:2

The most disgusting thing about pride is that it renders us unable to see ourselves clearly.

We deceive ourselves by thinking we are better than someone else. We deceive ourselves by thinking that we could not fall easily into traps of sin, by thinking that our essential goodness is good enough. God detests hubris. Think how difficult it must be to try to correct or warn a prideful person. God gives us ample warning to change our ways; to repent and turn to humility. If we don't humble ourselves before Him, He will do it . . . usually with a healthy dose of disgrace so we do not soon forget the lesson.

How much more graceful is a humble person? A humble person heeds good advice, is willing to review and alter their behavior where necessary, is able to apologize with sincerity, and can take criticism without becoming defensive or fragile.

Pride is deadly. We must fight it in earnest.

Open the Blinds of Unforgiveness

*Anyone who claims to be in the light
but hates his brother is still in the darkness.*

1 JOHN 2:9

Harboring resentment is living life in a dark cave. There is no comfortable place to sit, it is impossible to see, creepy things scurry around, the ceiling drips, and you are always cold.

There is a boulder blocking your exit from the cave—and it has the mighty weight of unforgiveness. Forgiveness is the one thing that seems impossible, yet it is required for freedom. The Lord knows our disdain for life in the cave (He wants so much beauty for us!), and He knows in our weakness that we cannot heave the boulder out of our way. He waits for us to get so sick of living in darkness and bondage that we finally do the only thing left—ask the Lord to help us move the boulder and reveal the light outside.

You know whom you need to forgive. You know what you need to let go of. It's time to roll the boulder aside and exit the cave. Ask for divine strength. He is happy to use His might on your behalf.

LEAVING ANGER IN CAPABLE HANDS

Contend, O Lord, with those who contend with me.

PSALM 35:1

We are all aware that it is against God's will to live a life of vengefulness and anger. We know that anger is poison, and we need to "let it go." We know all these things, yet when we are in pain we want to scream, "Yes! But HOW?"

There is nothing wrong with anger. Jesus experienced anger when He walked on this earth. But there is a major difference between being a person who is angry and being an angry person. If we aren't careful, one can lead to the other, and a temporary state becomes a permanent trait. By asking the Lord to contend with those who contend with us, we release our anger into capable hands.

His holy hands can seek appropriate justice while simultaneously ministering to our pain. We can truly "let it go" when we take ourselves out of the fray and trust Him to fight our battles on our behalf.

When we release interest in revenge, we can apply our energy to more important aspects of healing.

START WITH ONE THING

Do not repay evil with evil or insult with insult,
but with blessing, because to this you were called
so that you may inherit a blessing.

1 PETER 3:9

It is our natural inclination to retaliate or to get in the last word. Perhaps our methods of revenge include cold silence or an icy stare.

As Christians we are called to rise above our natural inclinations and see the face of Christ in all people and situations. We are called to do that which we are certain we cannot to.

Try it. Surprise yourself and surprise others who think they have you defined. Breathe when you would normally attack. Call someone when you would usually wait on them. React with forgiveness when you want to keep score. Soften when you feel rigid. Be kind when you want to scream. Call upon God's mercy to supply you with this supernatural grace.

Try today to do one thing differently and feel the immediate rush of the Spirit to a numb or aching place, like blood returning to a sleepy limb.

SEEK BEFORE YOU SPEAK

Set a guard over my mouth, O Lord;
keep watch over the door of my lips.
Let not my heart be drawn to what is evil.

PSALM 141:3–4

A little mystery can be a good thing.

Thoughts do not always deserve to be immediately translated into speech or action. Wise women are patient. Wise women are discreet. Wise women are refined. Not everyone needs to know what we are thinking. Let them wonder.

Meanwhile, the word of God is a wonderful sieve. We can develop the habit of straining our thoughts so that what is godly is presented to others and what is not worthy is turned over to God and released into His hands. Offering our minds to Christ is the first step to purifying our words and our behavior—ultimately, our character.

When you are uncertain if you should say or do something, pause. It is wiser to wait and seek before you speak. Haste is impatience that breeds mistakes.

Give the Holy Spirit a chance to guide you instead of relegating Him to the cleanup crew.

BEFORE AND AFTER

The Spirit of the Lord will come upon you in power . . .
and you will be changed into a different person.
1 SAMUEL 10:6

All our old ways will fade. All our defensiveness, rationalization, hiding, and usual patterns for dealing with people and situations will fall away.

Just when we think we have no hope of handling things differently, that we are stuck in a rut that has become our reality . . . the Spirit of the Lord will come upon us.

When we draw our insight and strength through the channel of God's power, everything changes—because He enables us to change. It will be an inside job. We will become a spiritual case study of "before and after." All the ways we have defined ourselves, all the ways that we have allowed others to define us, will fall away. All that remains is the way God defines us.

Notice when you can articulate yourself without fear or hiding. Notice when you have the composure to say nothing and stand firm in the confidence and conviction of your silence. Notice the way God is transforming you.

WHEN GOD PUTS YOU IN TIME-OUT

*I am now going to allure her; I will lead
her into the desert and speak tenderly to her.*

HOSEA 2:14

Even when God gives us a "talking-to," He does it with respect and sensitivity. When He leads us out into the desert, it is for the purpose of speaking to us alone—without others and without distraction. We can learn to come willingly . . . or we can be dragged out there, as He plies what we cling to from our desperate grasp.

He brings us to the desert for various reasons—to reprimand us, purify us, test us, prepare us, or teach us. The sooner we stop fighting our time in the sand, the sooner He can make His point or help shape us. He speaks tenderly to the core of our existence. Even if His news is not what we want to hear, we can take ultimate comfort that His words are exactly what we need to know.

READY TO HEAL

Do you want to get well?

JOHN 5:6

∂∞

Emotional difficulty or frailty can render us codependent like the spouse of an alcoholic.

In times of stark pain or betrayal, friends and family descend to caretake and comfort. It feels sweet and validating. If we are not careful and linger too long in this place, it can become intoxicating. Our codependency lies in tying our identity to our pain or circumstance. The world moves on. No one wants to continue to dress old wounds for you.

In a profound and timeless manner, Jesus questions the invalid in Jerusalem who had been ill for thirty-eight years: "Do you want to get well?"

Well, do you? Really? Are you holding on to old grudges and grievances or are you finally ready to move on?

Search your heart for the honest answer to this question. Find out if you are prepared to heal or if you have a perverse enjoyment in replaying your misfortune.

When you are sure you are ready, ask Jesus to come.

LIFE GOES ON

Then David got up from the ground.

2 SAMUEL 12:20

After seven days of fasting and praying to plead with God for the life of his son, David received the news that his son was dead.

The servants were afraid to tell David that the infant had died, especially in light of his weeklong display of agony. To their surprise, when David learned the news, he got up, dressed, went to the temple, and ate.

We all wrestle with God over certain things. We pray and plead, but sometimes God has other things in mind. When He gives His final answer, we need to think of David and be prepared to let go and move on.

It is good to go to great lengths to preserve something or someone of importance. It is important to fast and persevere in prayer. But if "no" is the answer, we must honor God's decision by moving on in the direction of His choosing.

THE CLOCK IS TICKING

If he comes suddenly, do not let him find you sleeping.
MARK 13:36

None of us really, truly like to think about our own mortality. Regardless of the depth of our faith and our belief in life everlasting, we still prefer to think of death in distant and impersonal terms. We would probably appreciate some advance warning so we could tend to some things we may have been neglecting.

The bottom line is that we do not know when the Lord will be coming for us. We may enjoy the peaceful winding-down of a long life, we may depart unexpectedly, we may battle an illness that leads to the end of our earthly story. Yet we do have advance warning; after all, He has let us know that He will come. Think of it as more prudent than morbid to set things in order.

Unsaid words, fractured relationships, withheld forgiveness, unmade amends . . . these are not deathbed items. We may never get a deathbed! These are important responsibilities of the living, not the dying.

Get to work.

COVERING YOUR LOSSES

I will repay you for the years the locusts have eaten.

JOEL 2:25

❧

Resist the temptation to despair or delve into disappointment. Yes, there has been loss. You may feel like you have forfeited years, opportunities, finances, and a significant return on investment of self. But hear the fantastic promise of redemption in Joel 2:25!

No one on earth can make anything up to you.

No one can pay.

No one can set things right or make things fair.

Pressure, manipulation, or guilt will not motivate justice, so the only option left is to let it go. Release the bitterness over what you have lost and allow God to fill your life with new blessings. If you are full of wrath, He cannot find space for His gifts and will be forced to return home with them.

God will make it up to you, and then some, if you keep an expectant attitude of faith. Thank Him that His promises are yours, are real and are already fulfilled. You will receive your first payment when you send your first thank-you note.

THE HONEST PATH

Love . . . rejoices with the truth.
1 CORINTHIANS 13:6

❧

"Listen, I need to tell you something that has been on my
    mind."

"You know, when you say things like that, I feel . . ."

"Did you just intend to hurt my feelings?"

"Yes, actually, I do need some space."

"I love you, but I can no longer tolerate your behavior when
    you . . ."

"I made a mistake and I need to tell you about it . . ."

Love needs truth to survive . . . and thrive. The hardest
words to say are often exactly what need to be spoken. As
afraid as we may be to open our hearts and speak the truth,
we should be more afraid of what happens when we do not.
When we hide the truth, bend the truth, or avoid the truth,
we begin the process of shutting down. This kills love,
bleeding out every last drop of its essence, leaving it empty
and dead.

Try today to speak your truth when you are tempted to
lie or downplay. Speaking the truth can begin as simply as
any other habit.

Sweet Silence

Without wood a fire goes out; without
gossip a quarrel dies down.
PROVERBS 26:20

It can be very tempting to vent.

It can be temporarily validating to air your dirty laundry.

Having the last word might seem like a victory.

But notice how quickly that righteous feeling turns to shame . . . usually faster than you can walk away, hang up the phone, or hit "send." The same way that following God's will provides a pleasant rush of Spirit, speaking out of turn can instantly wrap you in the chill of His displeasure.

Discretion brings peace. God will help you wash your dirty laundry, fold your clean clothes, and put them away— so share the load with Him. Let gossip die of malnutrition and suffocation.

I cannot emphasize enough how crucial it is to get control over your tongue. I wish someone had warned me, so I am warning you. Stop talking to everyone and start praying. Soon enough you will have pleasant words to share with strangers to enable you to speak wisdom and grant comfort to others.

STRENGTH IN WEAKNESS

[The Lord said,] "My grace is sufficient for you,
for my power is made perfect in weakness."
2 CORINTHIANS 12:9

≈

Nothing levels the field like humility.

A puffed-up, angry person lashes out, expecting defensiveness and wrath to mirror their own ugliness. This escalates, with each remark becoming more and more toxic until finally no one can breathe. Respond with a humble, vulnerable expression of softness, and the fire is instantly snuffed out.

There is nothing else to say, no more battle to fight.

Boasting about our weakness (I read as humility and softness) allows God to step in and take over with His grace. His power is perfected and illustrated in our inadequacy and subsequent release.

A reply like, "You know, you are right. I have a lot of work to do," or "Can you help me do a better job with that?" totally diffuses an ambush. You can quench a flame with a properly drawn boundary as well, for example, "I value your thoughts, but you seem too angry to discuss things peacefully right now. Can we talk later?"

Fight fire with water . . . living water.

SUCCESS IS RELATIVE

Be still before the Lord and wait patiently for him;
do not fret when men succeed in their ways,
when they carry out their wicked schemes.

PSALM 37:7

I can become punitive, childlike even, when I focus my attention on what I perceive to be fair or unfair. When I affix my own judgment or rely on my own evaluation of the situation, I roll out the red carpet to welcome discouragement and despair.

Fretting is a sin. It is not up to us to place value on circumstances or the actions of another. What may seem like present success may become eternal damnation. It may appear that someone is lucky or gets off the hook, but we have not read the final chapter. What appears to be luck one day can seem like a curse the next. We would do well to focus on our own yard, rather than peeking over the fence next door. Success in God's eyes should be what we are striving for.

How would it affect your sense of fairness to know that you will ultimately have eternal victory? The injustices and iniquities of this life are so temporal. Look to your finish line and live with eternity's values in mind.

STAY CLEAN

*It is God's will that by doing good you should
silence the ignorant talk of foolish men.*

1 PETER 2:15

You cannot win by entering a shouting match involving gossip or slander. An attempt to preserve your own reputation can dig another gaping hole, when you are trying to fill the first.

To practice silence and discretion in these kinds of situations is wise. Let God hear what you have to say and take up for you in His way. Energy spent trying to salvage your name and your position is wasted energy. At this point all energy needs to be focused on God. Work on being consistent and accountable. Let your actions promote God's name and His position.

The old cliché "Actions speak louder than words" has great merit. Follow Peter's advice and do good things. Let your behavior speak for you. Focus on God, not what other people are saying to you, about you, or behind your back. Concentrate only on doing God's will and stay clean.

Respect is the best silencer of all.

A MERCIFUL JUDGE

*The Father judges no one, but has
entrusted all judgment to the Son.*

JOHN 5:22

And how blessed are we?

If we were left with Old Testament standards, most of us would be in big trouble. There is no way to please God by the very nature of our humanity. Apart from following His laws, there would be no way we could receive His blessing. No matter how high we aim, we will always fall short of the mark of grace. Thankfully we are not judged by our own merit but by the merit of the One who loves us.

Praise God for His mercy and grace. Praise God for the redemption of the Cross. Praise God for delegating the responsibility of judgment to His compassionate Son. Praise God for the sacrifice of His Son so that we would even have the opportunity for everlasting life.

Nothing we do will ever be good enough. But rather than this statement being a cause for discouragement or malaise—let us be encouraged, humbled, and grateful. Let us acknowledge our smallness in the shadow of His greatness. What a relief to know we are covered.

CONFIDENCE THROUGH CHRIST

Do not be terrified; do not be afraid of them.
The Lord your God, who is going before you,
will fight for you, as he did for you in Egypt,
before your very eyes, and in the desert.

DEUTERONOMY 1:29–31

Are you aware that the God of the universe has your back?

Whether you are standing unarmed in front of those who want to steal your peace, or feeling utterly alone in the "desert" of your barren season . . . the Lord will fight for you. He will take up your cause. He will defeat those who challenge you. He will remove your spirit of fear and replace it with a spirit of courage and peace.

Look forward to your future with confidence. Not a confidence borne of self, but a Christ-centric confidence. We can take courage in the fact that He has promised never to leave or forsake us; therefore, we know that there is no trial we must face alone. He has gone before us, He stands behind us, and He is with us . . . all at once.

This message is from God to you:

"Do not be terrified.

Do not be afraid.

I have you, sweetheart."

DELAYED UNDERSTANDING

*As the heavens are higher than the earth, so
are my ways higher than your ways and my
thoughts higher than your thoughts.*

ISAIAH 55:9

One day Jesus will blindfold us like a little girl, grab our hand, and lead us into heaven. He will say, "SURPRISE!" and lift the blindfold, revealing everything.

All the things that made no sense will have crystal clarity. All the pain that felt unnecessary will become meaningful and dissipate like mist. All the loose ends will weave together perfectly. What we perceived as brokenness will be revealed as cracks caused by irrepressible growth. We will probably laugh when we reflect back on our totally incorrect perception of circumstances and our misunderstanding and mishandling of people.

It's not that we are stupid creatures. God gave us fine minds. It's just that we live within the limitations of being human. We are particularly constrained by our incomplete perspective from this side of heaven, and our minuscule part in the greatness of God's plan.

But what comfort to know that although we don't comprehend, He knows everything. We can rest in that instead of frantically trying to figure out now what is impossible to understand until later.

STEADY NOW

*The God of all grace . . . will himself restore
you and make you strong, firm and steadfast.*
1 PETER 5:10

An incredible promise, especially if you are feeling weak, wobbly, and uncertain.

Feelings are totally irrelevant in the face of God's power and grace. If we put too much stock in our emotions, we will ride a roller coaster that is destined to crash. Only by focusing on God can we overcome our emotions and be steadfast and strong in something bigger than ourselves. Sometimes it takes only a moment of prayer in the midst of turbulence: "Lord, things are starting to get rough. Instead of following my emotions, I am going to deliberately choose to follow You. I know You are in control, whether it feels like it or not. I believe I am safe in Your care. I pray in Your name, amen."

When we trust God instead of our feelings, by turning our situation over to Him, we allow Him to come into our weakness and restore us to grace.

Envision yourself as strong, firm, and steadfast. Claim that image as your new reality, based on the promise that God Himself will make it happen.

SEEKING HIM

*His divine power has given us everything
we need for life and godliness through
our knowledge of him who called us.*

2 PETER 1:3

I got into the trap of praying to God for answers and then tapping my feet and waiting for His response. As though the Creator of the universe owes me explanations or blessing! He owes me nothing, and I owe Him everything. He has given me life (present and eternal), redemption, freedom, and peace. Seek Him first, and all other things will be given to you.

I was blind to the wondrous fact that *I already had everything I needed*—it was all right here! The point isn't to pray to God to get to an answer . . . we pray to get to God Himself. If we seek Him first, not direction or blessing, everything else falls into place. He has equipped us mightily since He called our name.

Ask yourself this question: What would I be doing something differently if I knew I had everything I needed to make it happen?

Then do *that thing*, because you already have what it takes.

Too Good Not to Be True

Watch—and be utterly amazed. For I am going to do something in your days that you would not believe, even if you were told.

HABAKKUK 1:5

✌

Four years ago I was mired in misery. I felt hopeless, fearful, and anxiety-ridden. If the Lord had tried to tell me then what my life would look like today, I would never have believed Him.

From the bottom of the pit, my view was bleak. I never would have believed I would be here today—my kids are doing great, my faith has never failed me, I've completed four marathons as a new runner, have begun to realize my dream of writing as a career, and am dating someone special. Areas of desolation are showing signs of bloom.

Project your vision forward a few years and create what seems to be the most incredible, perfect, impossible scenario. Use all your creative thinking powers and imagine the best. Then try to grasp that your idea of best is not even a mediocre idea for God. Impossible to grasp? Yes. Our minds are not meant to understand the greatness of His understanding. Just know that no matter what you can conceive, God has something even greater in mind for you!

NEVER FORGET

You brought my life up from the pit,
O Lord my God . . . When my life was ebbing away,
I remembered you, Lord, and my prayer rose to you.

JONAH 2:6–7

I feel like I could have penned this Scripture. I credit God alone for lifting my life out of the pit. I finally "remembered" God when life as I knew it was ebbing away. How merciful is our Lord that He hears our prayers and spares us even after we have turned our back to Him countless times? The fact that He heard my prayers, forgave me my iniquities, and welcomed me home after I had blatantly ignored Him is proof that He is shepherding the lost sheep and celebrates our return to His fold.

Never again do I want to be so lost that I have forgotten God.

I don't want to remember Him at the last minute or go to Him as a last resort. I want Him front and center, as my first line of response and defense, the first person I talk to, the first arms I run to.

Lord, I will never forget my redemption from the pit. May it humble me forever.

TRUDGING FORWARD

Go ahead, march on.
2 SAMUEL 15:22

These words come from David's sad and resolute departure from Jerusalem, after his son Absalom betrayed him and took over his kingdom.

Even in the depths of our deepest sorrow and in the emptiness of our most wretched betrayal, Jesus never abandons us. He is beside us, footstep after footstep, as we go forward. Regardless of how bleak things look right now, He is already at work behind the scenes, setting things right.

As He did for David, the Lord will restore us to our former glory. He will take care of injustice and repair our damages over time. When we leave these big things to Him, we have enough energy and peace to tend to the immediate matters of life and family.

What is important right now is not that we try to figure out exactly where we're going . . . but simply that we go ahead and march on.

YOUR OWN RACE

*You shall not covet . . . anything that
belongs to your neighbor.*

EXODUS 20:17

My runner friend gave me a ceramic sign that reads simply "Run your own race."

I keep this by my desk as a reminder. In a race, it does not matter what any single person around you is doing. All that matters is that you know your own plan, go at your own pace, and compete only with yourself. That's why it's called a P.R.—personal record. It's between you and you.

God gives us all different gifts. If you are so busy looking at what your neighbor got, you will miss the gifts you have been given. By comparing yourself to others, you cease to be grateful for what you have because you are focusing on what you don't have. By coveting your neighbor's life, you are not living your own.

Keep your eyes straight ahead. You have to run your own race.

DIVINE VISION

*"What do you want me to do for you?" Jesus asked him.
The blind man said, "Rabbi, I want to see."*

MARK 10:51

You do realize that in a sense, all of us are "the blind man." Until we love and accept Christ, we all lack spiritual vision. The apostle Paul explains that we simply cannot comprehend spiritual truths until they are revealed to us by His Spirit (see 1 Cor. 2:10).

We can tell Jesus that we want to see. Every morning during my quiet time I ask the Lord to give me ears to hear and eyes to see. I want Him to know that I desire vision and wisdom, dispensed in His timing. Little by little, as we are ready, He will show us new things. It is important for our growth that we recognize our blindness, that we express our desire for vision, and that we prepare ourselves to receive and recognize what He reveals.

What did the blind man do when we could suddenly see? He started moving in the right direction!

Immediately he received his sight and followed Jesus along the road (v. 52).

Watch the Road

Devote yourselves to prayer, being watchful and thankful.
COLOSSIANS 4:2

We've all done it . . . driving along, thinking we are totally in the clear; we slide over to change lanes only to be surprised with a loud, long honk and an angry driver swerving next to us. Yep . . . a blind spot.

Spiritually, we are no different. We all have blind spots, no matter how far we have come or how hard we try. We all have things about ourselves that we just can't recognize or don't want to recognize. Often these blind spots are our weak areas that can quickly get us into big trouble—just like pulling in front of another driver.

What do we do about our blind spots if we are blind to them? Number one, we pray about them, because often this humble desire to grow invites God to reveal them to us. Number two, we find a group of Christian women to study and grow with. In their company we can safely work on the hard stuff, building trust and confidence along the way.

Restored Faith in Love

This is my prayer: that your love may abound
more and more in knowledge and depth of insight,
so that you may be able to discern what is best.

PHILIPPIANS 1:9–10

As Paul prayed for the Philippians, I now pray these words for you.

You may feel that your capacity to love is diminished or broken. It may be, if you look at love from outside in. But the Lord's abounding love begins inside, in the deep and wounded places of the soul. When your knowledge and insight are based in truth, you learn to choose wisely, to discern what is best, and to live and love without fear.

This healing begins within and radiates out in the form of abounding love. It can only be experienced, not explained.

Don't go sour. Don't settle for less than a healed heart. Don't stop believing.

It really matters that you still believe in love.

THE LAST WORD

You were shown these things so that you might know that the Lord is God; besides him there is no other.

DEUTERONOMY 4:35

The Lord is God, and He has the final say on all matters.

We can pray for anything that is on our hearts, but only God knows what is ultimately best for us and for His perfect plan. Two instances in the New Testament illustrate God responding to a request with the answer "No." Paul asks for the thorn to be removed and God says, "My grace is sufficient for you." This taught Paul about humility and dependence (and now teaches us).

And in the Garden of Gethsemane, Jesus asks His Father if the cup can pass from Him and gets a "No." This response led to the highest act of love and obedience, which ultimately saved the world.

How does Jesus respond to "no"? He accepts it with grace. "*Not my will but yours.*" That is the place we must aim for in our relationship with God. We know we can ask for anything, but His word is the final say.

Pray to desire His will more than your own.

HUMILITY BRINGS FREEDOM

*Now Moses was a very humble man, more humble
than anyone else on the face of the earth.*

NUMBERS 12:3

Moses had reason to be arrogant. God spoke directly to him, in *conversation*, not in visions, dreams, or riddles. Pretty impressive, if you ask me. And yet, Moses was more humble than anyone else on earth.

Why?

Moses possessed the secret strength of humility. Humility is not placing yourself beneath others, shuffling along all meek and lowly. Not at all. Humility is knowing *who you are in relation to God.*

Yes, I am a tiny, powerless ant on the face of creation compared to His omnipotence. But (and this is important) *I am something special because He loves me.* My value is in the fact that I am loved, not that I am worthy of love.

When you begin to understand the role humility plays in cultivating unshakable confidence, you will be well on your way to freedom.

PEACE IS PERSONAL

*If it is possible, as far as it depends on you,
live at peace with everyone.*

ROMANS 12:18

"If it is possible"?—All things are possible with God! We have no excuse or escape clause.

"As far as it depends on you," meaning, it does not matter how the other person acts, what they say, or what choices they make. We have the ability to choose a path of peace for ourselves. That choice, once made, cannot be altered by anyone. It is powerfully personal. My friend Ann always tells me to "triangulate," meaning, take what you cannot resolve directly with someone to the Lord and allow Him to resolve it for you. Put the impossible where it belongs, leave it alone, and do not break peace.

It sounds impossible or improbable to live at peace with everyone, until we remember that we have responsibility for only ourselves! There is immense freedom in that. We choose to keep our peace and that's it—we act accordingly, and our part is complete.

Someone else's lack of peace is between them and God.

SEEKING VS. SEEING

*You will seek me and find me when you
seek me with all your heart.*

JEREMIAH 29:13

After all our earnest looking and seeking, we find the Lord was right with us all along. Perhaps all this time it wasn't that we were blind but that we had too many things blocking our view.

Seeing clearly is a matter of vision and vista. This equates to perception and perspective. Our eyes need to be taught to see, and they need to be taught what to look for. Seeking involves more of a stretch than simply seeing.

Like symphony music or a nice glass of wine, this Scripture ends on a very fine note. "I will change your lot," says the Lord.

What an incredible piece of news. I am here with you, and I will change your circumstances. If we faithfully wait on the Lord, listen to Him, and carry out His instructions, our lives are headed for redemption. All our pain and despair will soon be exchanged for joy and peace.

Unforeseen Options

Moses stretched out his hand over the sea,
and all that night the Lord drove the sea back . . .
The waters were divided.

EXODUS 14:21

Have you felt trapped? Like there is literally no clear way out of your current mess? Stop thinking, manipulating, and running around . . . and start praying.

The Lord will provide a way out, most likely in a powerful way that has never entered your mind as an option. Think of the Israelites, trying to flee the Egyptian army. They arrive at the sea with Pharaoh's forces on their tails.

They probably had a serious moment of discouragement, looking from one direction to the other. But then God stepped in and split the sea to permit their crossing. (Do you think they considered that as an option?) And just as the Egyptians followed, the sea closed around them. Think today of the powerful provision and protection evidenced in this story and know that God will do the same for you. When you arrive at and acknowledge the limit of everything you know, He can begin to apply what He knows.

The Hidden Blessing

*Every day I will praise you and extol
your name for ever and ever.*

PSALM 145:2

As much as I would like to sometimes, I cannot simply put the kids directly into bed and enjoy my quiet house at the end of a long day. There is a process involved that I affectionately call "Bed, Bath, and Beyond." It's a time to clean up, settle down, listen to a story, and snuggle.

We need to give God some time before drifting off to sleep. Just like children need some quiet time with a parent to settle them to sleep—so do we, with our heavenly Father.

We can take a few minutes to reflect over our day, and review and confess things as needed. This reflection enables us to see ourselves more clearly over time, and helps us to truly attempt to do better each day.

When times are dark, reflecting over a hard day is not pleasant. But we must get into the practice of finding the blessing. Every day He will bless us. The blessing may be small or camouflaged, but we can refine our sense of vision and gratitude in the search.

THE WISDOM OF WAITING

Yet the Lord longs to be gracious to you; he rises to show you compassion. For the Lord is a God of justice. Blessed are all who wait for him.

ISAIAH 30:18

We talk a lot about cultivating a spirit of patience and learning to wait on the Lord. But we rarely think that the Lord also waits on us.

He stands at the door like a spiritual benefactor, His arms laden with gifts and blessings. He waits until we are ready to receive. He waits for the perfect moment. He waits until we appreciate what we are asking for. He waits until we have made sufficient preparations in our heart. He waits until we are not too busy to notice. He waits until we are clean and free from resentment and discontent. He waits to answer until we have fully understood our question.

He waits until our maturity is appropriate and our understanding is elevated. He waits until our arms are open and unhindered. Sometimes He waits until we think He has forgotten, just to test and grow our faith. It's not just a matter of waiting, but waiting wisely.

SUSTAINABLE JOY

Your joy will be complete.
DEUTERONOMY 16:15

The inspiring author Anne Lamott writes the following beautiful expression in one of her books: "Peace is joy at rest."

When "our joy is complete" is perhaps when our heart is at peace, resting. Maybe peace is a more advanced and sustainable phase of joy. Think of a woman who possesses this quiet, resting joy. It bubbles like champagne under the surface of her being, threatening to effervesce—in a smile, a laugh, a hug, or a kind remark. You want to be where she is, even if it's the grocery store.

It's that kind of mature joy that makes people wonder, "What is it with her?" or "How does she get more beautiful instead of just getting older?" It's something difficult to discern for those who do not have the peace of the Lord in their hearts. To live this way is a living, teaching example to everyone around us—both friends and strangers.

Meditate on this idea of resting joy.

KEEPING TABS ON ANGER

Do not let the sun go down while you are still angry,
and do not give the devil a foothold.

EPHESIANS 4:26–27

Anger is not a sin. It is a valid reading on the spectrum of human emotion. It is our barometer of injustice. It is sometimes the impetus for great change. It can be the fuel of self-preservation.

But we are instructed in Scripture to manage our anger, and this means our anger cannot manage us. We are not to sin in our anger, so we can feel the emotion but not necessarily act on the emotion. We are also taught to limit the duration of the experience, not to go to sleep with an angry heart. This is so simple and yet such grand instruction. Going to bed with anger gives this nasty spirit an opportunity to fester, grow, and explore other areas of our being while we sleep unmonitored. We will awake in a fitful, unrested, sour state, and the enemy will have successfully poisoned another day intended to be lived in freedom for God's glory.

Don't let him.

CHECK YOUR LUGGAGE

When they looked for him, he was not to be found . . . And the Lord said, "Yes, he has hidden himself among the baggage."

1 SAMUEL 10:21–22

Just when I think I have successfully hidden from everyone and quarantined myself with my own sin, sorrow, or bad mood, the Lord calls me out.

"There she is, over there, attempting to hide in her baggage," He says.

And I thought I was so clever! Perhaps I should get rid of some of the baggage to make hiding more difficult? The people who love me always manage to find me, especially when the Lord blatantly points me out. There is nowhere to go where I can stray too far. There is nowhere to hide where I am unseen. The eyes of the Lord are omniscient. He instructs us to travel light, yet we persist in overpacking carry-on bags and dragging suitcases behind us. He forgives all our sins, yet we continue to carry our old burdens.

Today is a perfect day to get rid of some baggage and make it harder to hide.

SUBMISSION BRINGS CLARITY

Everyone must submit himself.
ROMANS 13:1

It's funny that it takes more courage to be dependent than independent. It's ironic that it takes more strength to submit our lives than it does to fight for them. Why is releasing more grueling than struggling to hang on?

We must submit ourselves. Not just once, but daily, moment by moment, decision by decision. I pray every morning for guidance and wisdom. I pray that the Lord will clear my muddy waters by whatever way He sees fit . . . even if it is by process of elimination. I pray to Him to take things and people away that are not of Him. And by this removal, I pray that I will be able to see the important, intended things with more clarity and reverence.

Submission is an act of trust. We must trust the Lord to remove and reorganize things as He wishes . . . even if it is painful, we must know that He knows best.

THE HOLY GARDENER

*"I will plant Israel in their own land, never
again to be uprooted from the land I have
given them," says the LORD your God.*

AMOS 9:15

❧

Like a plant too long constrained in the same pot, our roots
can become bound and twisted into a tight clump. Over
time we are unable to be fully nourished and cannot grow
beyond the limits of our environment.

Divorce can be a necessary replanting. It is an opportunity to establish deep roots and realize our potential outside
our previous container.

Allow the Lord to replant you. Let Him gently remove
you and expose your captivity. Let Him find the perfect
place for you and tenderly place you properly and begin to
nourish you. Your roots will extend into the rich soil of your
newfound freedom.

If the Lord replants you according to His will, you will
not be uprooted again. He does not make mistakes.

RENOVATIONS

*The Lord declares to you that the Lord
himself will establish a house for you.*

2 SAMUEL 7:11

Divorce can make you feel like your home has toppled like a house of cards . . . like everything you have worked so hard to build is a total sham. And, unfortunately, it may have been a sham if it was built on a foundation other than God. It's a discouraging and frightening experience to know you have so much to rebuild but no idea where to start. But starting over offers a unique opportunity to do it right.

If you put the Lord first, He promises that He will establish your house. He will rebuild it in every way . . . financially, literally, emotionally, spiritually. He will restore you to where you were and bless you in abundance beyond that. He has a master plan for you. He knows exactly where you are today and the good things He has in store for you tomorrow.

Trust Him to establish your home.

OPEN HANDS

Offer right sacrifices and trust in the Lord.

PSALM 4:5

Sacrifices are not something conceptually restricted to Old Testament times—like the burning of animals to appease God's wrath or receive His forgiveness. Right sacrifices come in many forms and are as relevant today as always. The Lord may call on us to release something in order to test our willingness to obey him or to purify our hearts. He may call on us to do something in order to actively atone for our shortcomings. He may call on us to offer something, to give of ourselves when we think we're empty.

Sometimes we must give up certain foods, certain attitudes, certain habits, certain resentments, even certain relationships in order to honor God more fully in our lives. When the Holy Spirit prompts us to give or give up something in His name, we must trust in His wisdom to know what is best.

We must never hold on to anything so tightly that we cannot free our grip to grasp God's hand.

From Barrenness to Bounty

*Sing, O barren woman . . . For your Maker is
your husband the Lord Almighty is his name.*

ISAIAH 54:1, 5

A barren woman is not just a woman unable to conceive a
child. She is a woman unable to conceive a future for herself. She is without hope and without direction. She is emotionally desolate, unable to bear spiritual fruit.

I have had moments of profound emptiness like this,
feeling futile and alone. In those moments, we can encourage
ourselves by remembering that we are far from alone, a far cry
from empty. We are in the presence of the Trinity, filled with
the Holy Spirit. When an earthly husband steps out, the
Lord steps in. As always, He sees a need and He fills it. He
can take us from places of desolation to places of beauty and
bounty. He can make our lives fertile and hopeful.

We can and must rejoice in this gift. We should raise a
glad cry that we are being redeemed from barren places, in
preparation to bear great fruit.

Spiritual Boomerang

As you have done, it will be done to you;
your deeds will return upon your own head.
OBADIAH 1:15

Every day is a series of choices.

We can choose to feel certain emotions, or not.

We can choose to act upon our feelings, or not.

We can choose action or patience, words or silence, to offer or to draw back, to retaliate or to turn a cheek, to help or to ignore, to propagate peace or to assist anger.

Our choices have a boomerang effect, bringing us amounts of peace or blessing equal to that which we offer the world. When we choose to speak or to act, it should be a prayerful and purposeful decision. When we seek God first in our day, we can go forward with confidence knowing that He is with us each moment. When we submit our choices to Him for guidance and blessing, we know we will not step unsafely outside His will. Reaping and sowing are the holy system of balance. We yield a crop from the seeds we sow. May it be seeds of peace.

POTENTIAL BLOOM

You are a garden locked up, my sister, my bride;
you are a spring enclosed, a sealed fountain.

SONG OF SONGS 4:12

This particular book of the Bible is totally passionate and romantic. When I apply some of the Scripture as if it were Jesus speaking to me, I am overwhelmed. We (you and I) are His sisters, His brides. He loves and longs for us in such a way that would utterly melt our hearts if we could only understand it more fully.

He is speaking to us about the woman He sees within us, the potential for the woman He created us to be. Critical to becoming this great beauty and realizing our true potential is the acceptance of Christ's unconditional love.

He sees the impending bloom of the locked garden, the refreshment of the inner spring, and the pleasant sound of the running fountain. He knows how we are inhibited and closed and desires to set us all free with His great love.

COUNTING ON HIM

*Will he not bring to fruition my salvation
and grant me my every desire?*

2 SAMUEL 23:5

This faithful attitude of expectancy, when it is coming from a place of humble trust—not arrogance—pleases God. He loves to see our dependency and enjoys when we express our need for Him. When our hearts are soft, we are in a position to receive His guidance and blessings.

When we look to our Father with the trusting simplicity of a child, we can say with sparkling belief and a fresh voice, "I know You love me. I know You are coming for me. I can't wait to see what You are planning for me. You are so good to me. I love You."

This expectant, hopeful spirit gives the Lord plenty of room to work in our lives. It gives Him full access to exceed all our expectations. It takes the roadblocks of discouragement and unbelief out of His way. We stop limiting Him with our petty perspectives. Our expression of faith allows us to receive the good things God has for us.

TIME IS RELATIVE

With the Lord a day is like a thousand years,
and a thousand years are like a day.
2 PETER 3:8

≈

I remember being a child on a family road trip, thinking a day felt like a thousand years. I remember being a new mom, holding my sleeping baby boy, thinking that with him a thousand years would feel like a day.

Time is so relative . . . some days fly by and others tick and crawl. We all have an equal amount of time in any given day—twenty-four hours. Yet why do we make excuses like, "I just don't have time . . ." (to pray, to return a call, to see a friend, to work out, to read, to study, to go to church, etc.)? We always have time; we just don't always prioritize that time.

The Lord's sense of time is also relative; He has eternity as His backdrop. With ways and thoughts much higher than ours, He works things out by His own methodology. He can solve a problem in a minute, or in two generations.

Pray to God to bless your time . . . that you spend it wisely and well in accordance with His perfect will.

Hope in What Counts

*Command those who are rich in this present
world not . . . to put their hope in wealth, which
is so uncertain, but to put their hope in God.*

1 TIMOTHY 6:17

This passage is about more than money. "Riches" and "wealth" can also be defined as good times in every facet of life . . . finances, career, friendships, family, and love.

For me it's easier to be spiritually fit in times of suffering. In times of abundance, it takes more discipline not to be caught up in things that are so uncertain. It's interesting for me now to look back. The times I was most rich by worldly standards are the times I was the most empty. The times I seemed to have it all were the times I didn't have much. And all the while I didn't even recognize it; I was spiritually blind.

Our times of smooth sailing can be disrupted in a mere second, by one wave. This is why it is so important not to become distracted in pleasant times and to maintain our hope in God.

He is the only thing certain.

OPEN MY EYES

*Whatever was to my profit I now consider
loss for the sake of Christ.*

PHILIPPIANS 3:7

It's amazing how blind we can be and how easily we can be deceived. We can live our whole lives placing value in the wrong places. Our perception can be totally warped, thinking things are good for us when they are actually taking us down a path of destruction. Or thinking things are bad for us when they are actually the catalyst for our redemption.

Perhaps we should avoid prematurely assigning value to people and circumstances until we are more spiritually mature. More time spent in the company of the Lord and His teachings will allow us access to His views. We will begin to learn that the significance of any trial cannot be derived from its surface. In our life experience ledger of profit and loss we may be surprised at how often we have the columns reversed.

Lord, help us to submit our situations to You instead of evaluating them for ourselves.

BLESS THEM

*As for me, far be it from me that I should sin
against the Lord by failing to pray for you.*
1 SAMUEL 12:23

Since Christ is love, we know that love knows no conditions and has no end. Even if a relationship is severed, love does not disappear. Love is patient, kind, and enduring.

Even if someone causes us deep pain, we are instructed to bless them, not curse them. No matter how forced it feels at first, the more you persevere in prayer for someone who has hurt you, something remarkable happens. Although the person never knows of our intercession and perhaps we see no evidence of change in him or her, there comes a miraculous change within ourselves.

Places of resentment get fresh air and a more godly perspective. Soon enough this prayer is not forced at all, but a gift given freely and gladly. Eventually we begin to understand that in some form, despite our frequent inability to recognize it, love remains.

ETERNAL FOCUS

Since, then, you have been raised with Christ,
set your hearts on things above.
COLOSSIANS 3:1

Do you remember walking on a balance beam as a child? Walking above the ground on a thin platform, our inclination is to want to curl into ourselves and stare at our feet with each step. Nothing will make us fall more quickly than focusing on ourselves. The best way to traverse a balance beam is to hold our arms out and focus on something beyond the end of the beam. Our Christian walk is just like that; we make steady progress by holding our arms out to others and focusing our eyes on God.

If we allow our hearts to remain focused on present circumstances in this life, we fall captive to a dangerously limited perspective. When we are in pain, it can be annoying to hear a loved one remind us that "this too shall pass," or "one day this will be a vague memory." Annoying, possibly, but very wise.

These are fleeting times, even though time seems to expand in suffering. We are living a blip on the spectrum of eternity. Our experiences, while very serious to us in the moment, are a tiny precious component of God's kingdom plan.

Keep your focus on God.

UNEXPECTEDNESS OF ANSWERED PRAYER

*The Spirit intercedes for the saints in
accordance with God's will.*
ROMANS 8:27

I love that last scene in *Under the Tuscan Sun*, where Diane Lane is hosting a wedding at her Italian villa. Earlier in the movie she emotionally states how she wanted to see a wedding, a baby, and a family in that house.

A wise friend points out to her that there is indeed a wedding (not her own), a baby (her friend's), and a family (a tight group of friends). This revelation causes her to sit and shut her eyes at the wonder of it all.

It is often this way when we realize prayers have been answered. These answers may not come in the time or fashion that we intended, but God has His own purposes in mind. We need to put as much time into recognizing answered prayers and praising God as we do in making our requests.

It is unfolding all around you.

GOING SOLO

[Jesus] withdrew again to a mountain by himself.
JOHN 6:15

It is crucial to have fellowship with other believers. I believe we women need other spiritual women to maintain accountability and authenticity in our journey with the Lord.

We need church, shared prayer, and Bible study. These are external components to our growth in faith. However, we also need the internal component of quiet time spent alone with God.

We must clear the way to make this communion possible since it is the spring that feeds into all our rivers and fountains. Without it, we will eventually run dry. Jesus is our example of perfection. For all His time spent with the people, He always made time to get away. He needed space, even from His chosen and beloved disciples. We need to heed His example and maintain our private time with our Father . . . time not only for speaking, but also for listening.

Listening requires quietness and concentration. Go into the hills alone.

LASTING LOVE

*Live a life of love,
just as Christ loved us.*

EPHESIANS 5:2

❧

In our world today, love is overly romanticized and our expectations are pumped with false pretenses. We are such a disposable society that we find it easier and more convenient to throw a relationship away than to do the work required to sustain and protect love.

Lasting love is not about feelings; it's about commitment. It's about sticking it out when you feel like peeling out.

Our example of love is Christ. In Him we see that suffering is a part of love. In fact, it is how love is grown and perfected. Jesus shows us that the ultimate display of love is not emotion but self-sacrifice.

Mature love is fortified by each small gesture of self-sacrifice, in showing more concern for the greater good than for individual fulfillment. Meditate on our example of love.

STEP ASIDE

A man reaps what he sows.
GALATIANS 6:7

I can review my life and chart the holy patterns of sowing and reaping: sacrifice, kindness, or forgiveness yielding fruit down the line; or sin and resentment yielding pain and disappointment. God is just in His dealings with me.

I have considered sowing and reaping in terms of personal actions and choices in my own life. Only this year have I considered this law in terms of other people, and my relative role, which is, "Get out of the way."

Too often in a guise of compassion or self-importance we step in and get in God's way. It is one thing to offer prayer or comfort, another thing to meddle in God's lesson plan for another soul. This affects the way we help our families and friends, the way we discipline and raise our children, and the way we view our role in marriage and relationships.

We need to focus on sowing our own good crops, and not inhibit the spiritual growth of others. We must allow them to reap what they have sown.

THANK GOD

I will extol the Lord at all times; his praise
will always be on my lips.
PSALM 34:1

Time spent in quiet reflection and meditation with God yields a grateful spirit.

When I tend to my relationship with the Lord, I feel connected to Him all day—not only in my quiet time. All day long I am filled with praise. I notice His hand in everything. The subtle things that go unnoticed when I am disconnected from my source, become as personal as a handwritten love note and as evident as recognizing my own hands. The Lord speaks to me all day when I tune in to His channel.

The smile of my child.

A great parking place.

An unexpected call from an old friend.

A hug.

A beautiful day in the middle of winter.

A striking sunset.

An unplanned extra thirty minutes.

In all these things, from the minute to the life-changing moments, I want to say, "Thank You, Lord," out loud.

And I do.

REMEMBER HIS POWER

The Lord is a warrior; the Lord is his name.

EXODUS 15:3

We have all kinds of sweet and soft sentiments about Jesus. And rightly so, because He is gentle, compassionate, merciful, nonviolent, loving, and forgiving.

But He is not only sweet.

He is also a mighty warrior, the Ruler of the entire universe, and He wields the most powerful sword of all.

Never underestimate Jesus.

Do not view Him in a limited light.

Understand that He is at the right hand of God, presiding over everything. When you need saving, when you need protection, when you need the power of a hundred armies to fight for you . . . call upon the Lord.

PASSENGER SEAT

Then Jesus came to them and said, "All authority in heaven and on earth has been given to me."

MATTHEW 28:18

❧

Nothing can touch us that has not passed through the Lord first. So even when things seem to be spiraling out of our control, they are under His control. When we feel we have lost our place and our balance; He is in charge of restoring our position and equilibrium.

We look around and see how things grow and continue in nature and in the world. As the conductor of the universe, His hand is orchestrating it all.

When things are too much for us, it is a sign to kick back and get comfortable to wait on the Lord. We need to move to the backseat and let Him drive.

It is better to see what happens next when He is invited to reign in our circumstances, than to get into a frenzy of lamely trying to control them ourselves.

A Covenant Relationship

*I will betroth you to Me forever; . . . in righteousness
and justice, in love and compassion. I will betroth you
in faithfulness, and you will acknowledge the Lord.*

HOSEA 2:19–20

The word *betroth* is used primarily in the context of marriage. When an earthly marriage fails, it does not mean we are alone. Scripture refers to Christ as our Bridegroom and we are His brides, and what a lovely mate He is. Hear the attributes of our covenant relationship:

Forever, righteousness, justice, love, compassion, and faithfulness.

What more could a woman want? If you were going to write your own wedding vows, could you find more descriptive or appropriate words? Could you find a mate better equipped to honor those vows and help you honor them?

He desires such intimacy with us so that we know Him, and His Father, the way a wife knows her husband when marriage is realized to its full beauty, intent, and potential. It is said a woman is most beautiful when she is in love.

We are betrothed to Jesus. Revel in that proposal today.

REMEMBER BEING PLAYFUL?

*[The Lord] satisfies your desires with good things
so that your youth is renewed like the eagle's.*
PSALM 103:5

What is it that makes you feel young?

For my friend Paige, it is galloping at top speed across an open field on the back of a horse. For me, it is feeling sun and breeze on my face, sand on my feet, and the sound of surf crashing in my ears. In that moment, I am ageless.

I am a child chasing the tide or building elaborate sandcastles, a teenager writing the name of my summer boyfriend in the sand, a young woman in a floppy hat— pregnant with my first child and walking slowly with one hand on my belly, a mother watching my three children play, an old freckled woman reading a novel . . . I am all these things at once.

God knows this ageless place in you because He created it. It's the playground of your soul. Remember it?

Go and play and be renewed.

ALLURE

If any of them do not believe the word, they may be won over without words by the behavior of their wives.

1 PETER 3:1

It is heart-wrenchingly painful to live in a household that is not united in Christ. Trying to make life and maintain love with an unbeliever is like rowing upstream alone.

Being persuasive has no significance in bringing someone to faith. As women we must be alluring, not pushy. Our behavior shown to our husband, ex-husband, or in any relationship should speak loudly without words. A gentle spirit, a peaceful demeanor, a forgiving heart, and an inspired sense of morality are some of the features of a godly woman.

Even if a marriage is severed, it does not mean that the effect of a godly (ex) wife is diminished. We will always have some role to play in the spiritual journeys of the men in our lives. God created women to be alluring, to invite others into His presence.

Because you are no longer together does not mean you are off the hook. Live well.

THE DOORMAN

*What he opens no one can shut, and what
he shuts no one can open.*

REVELATION 3:7

His voice tells us, "This is the way, walk in it." We can continue down the long hallway with confidence, knowing as we pass doors and corridors that the ones intended for us will swing open.

If we align ourselves with God's will through prayer and study, we can be sure that we are taking responsibility for our own preparedness and readiness. We are working on our part, and surely the Lord will do His.

He opens doors for us that we never considered possible. He will create options where we see dead ends. He will shut doors abruptly, according to His plan, and prevent us from falling into traps. His ways cannot be changed. When it is His hand opening the door, no one can shut you out. When His hand forces the closing, we need to get out of His way.

THE FOOTHOLD OF DECEPTION

Encourage one another daily, . . . so that
none of you may be hardened by sin's deceitfulness.

HEBREWS 3:13

Sin is so deceptive and the voice of the enemy is so alluring and conniving that if we are not constantly vigilant, we will begin to stray from our path.

It begins with an instance of moral laziness or some inane, seemingly harmless curiosity. This is all the enemy needs to gain a foothold. His deception is malignant; it divides and spreads unbeknownst to the faltering host.

Then one small lie begets another and shadows darken into obscurity. We are conflicted by the constant tugging of our conscience trying to warn us of imminent danger. Because we inherently know how our sin grieves God, our hearts harden in response. This hardening of our hearts is a sure sign we are captive to the spirit of deception in some area(s). Pray to God to keep your heart and your eyes and ears open.

CAN IT BE?

Nothing is impossible with God.
LUKE 1:37

When Mary received the amazing news of her pregnancy, it was compounded by news of her cousin Elizabeth. Elizabeth, who was older and had been unable to have children in her youth, was six months pregnant!

Naturally, I am sure Mary was shocked by the series of implausible newsflashes. The response of the angel summed up her questioning nature, and our own, saying, "Nothing is impossible with God."

The next time you are tempted to speak words of self-doubt, recognize that the spirit of negativity does not come from God. Things like, "I can't do that," or "I'm not good at that," or "You really should ask someone else," or "That's impossible" are all LIES. Like Elizabeth, regardless of our age or circumstances, barren areas of our lives can and will be in bloom . . . expectant and full.

Use this Scripture to combat the lies in your head.

FROM FEAR TO FAITH

Faithful is He who calls you, and He
also will bring it to pass.
1 THESSALONIANS 5:24

When it comes to faithfulness—we all fall short.

Our faith has weak spots because our trust is limited by fear, which can be overcome only by love. If we have difficulty accepting His love because of a failed marriage, it impacts our level of fear, which in turn depletes our trust and inhibits our faith.

How great is God's divine mercy that His blessings and His ability and desire to uphold His promises are not based on our faithfulness—but on *His* faithfulness. Thankfully our belief is not the catalyst, His power is. He is exceedingly able to offer His strength in exchange for our weakness. His love erases fear, which builds the trust needed to have faith. And from a standpoint of restored faithfulness, He is able to work in us.

He teaches by example, not by coercion or punishment. He is a lavishly generous Father, not a withholding one. He will bring His will to pass in our lives. He will undeniably work *all things* together for our good.

LEARNING HOW TO ASK

Ask and it will be given to you.
MATTHEW 7:7

Like the cartoons with the genie in the bottle, this Scripture invites us to make a wish. If you had only one wish, what would it be?

Wisdom? To make sense of the senseless.

Peace? To quiet your restless spirit.

Healing? To mend your brokenness.

Forgiveness? For a second chance.

Love? To make everything worthwhile.

Whatever we ask, as long as our hearts are right before the Lord, we can expect our prayers to be answered. We would do well to spend more time formulating and understanding our questions than trying to predict how God will answer them. We would grow remarkably faster by focusing on the preparatory work of the heart that precipitates receiving. We would appreciate the resolution much more deeply if we uprooted our resentment to cultivate an atmosphere of gratitude. There is no question that the Lord will give, but will we be ready to receive?

MOVING FREELY

*Where these have been forgiven, there is
no longer any sacrifice for sin.*

HEBREWS 10:18

Once we have truly repented, our sins are immediately cast from us—as far as the east is from the west.

After this point, God no longer remembers our sin. Our spiritual slates are clean.

Why, then, do we persevere in carting around the heavy load of remembered sin? We hang on to things that God has released. Perhaps it is our lack of belief, or our lack of trust that prevents us from enjoying liberty. Or perhaps we enjoy taunting ourselves because we don't believe we are who God says we are.

Jesus died so that Christians could live victorious, reconciled, liberated, joyful, productive, and beautiful lives. Give thanks to the Lord for your clean slate by enjoying the freedom He died for. Let go of your past sins, and put the load down. You have been forgiven.

YOU ARE INTACT

Let love and faithfulness never leave you;
bind them around your neck, write them
on the tablet of your heart.

PROVERBS 3:3

An inscription on the heart is the most precious, intimate promise. What is bound around your neck? Hopefully it's something that reminds you, and points others, to God. A cross necklace reminds me of Christ's loving sacrifice for me. I often find myself touching mine when I am in the middle of a difficult moment or conversation, taking comfort in knowing who is with me.

Even if you feel like love and faithfulness have left you, they have not. Love and faithfulness are traits and gifts of God, and they do not depart. Love and faithfulness dwell within you. No one can take them from you, and no one can alter them. They are just as intact as they were at your creation. If you believe otherwise, you are being deceived.

Ask God to show you what is written on your heart—He will know because He wrote the words there Himself. Revel in the truth that you are completely intact.

ALL EYES ON HIM

The eye is the lamp of the body.
MATTHEW 6:22

In order to have lightness of being, we must seek light in every situation.

Since our eyes illuminate our bodies, we cannot allow our lenses to be clouded. Keeping a clear lens requires a commitment to truth and purity. The Word of God is our lens cleaner, polishing away the smudges and the dirt.

We must train ourselves to look for the good in every person and situation. Our eyes can be trained to find Christ in all things. With eyes of faith we can see hope and light even in the midst of clouds. We must constantly discipline ourselves to look away from darkness. If the eye is the lamp of the body—think how we pollute ourselves by looking at sin. Even if we are not actively participating, merely looking at it dims our spirits.

Lord, help us today to train our eyes on You—with absolute focus.

ENDURANCE

*Dear friends, build yourselves up in your
most holy faith and pray in the Holy Spirit . . .
Keep yourselves in God's love.*

JUDE 20–21

One of my favorite things about running marathons is that you can tell nothing about a runner by looking at them. Age, shape, weight, and attitude—none of it matters. Race day is race day. What matters is if you have done the work to be prepared, if God's favor is upon you, and if your spirit and body have been equally trained in endurance.

A mismatch between body and spirit will yield a poor finish. When the body subsides, the spirit (far more powerful) takes over. Endurance is built through experience, repeatedly practicing the effort so that you have what it takes to reach completion. Endurance is the confidence that you can withstand pain.

It is exactly the same in our spiritual "race." Better to be diligent and humble than to compare ourselves to others. We must focus on our own training—building ourselves up in our most holy faith.

A GENEROUS HEART

Give, and it will be given to you.
A good measure, pressed down, shaken together
and running over, will be poured into your lap.

LUKE 6:38

In the marketplaces of ancient times, customers preferred merchants who gave them a fair deal. This would mean a full sack of grain for the price paid. And yet the Lord goes beyond a full pour. He talks about proportions that are pressed down, filled to capacity, and overflowing beyond. Apply this Scripture to your heart, not just to your finances. A generous giver gives freely, with no thought to limits of payback.

When in pain, it is our instinct to turn inward and turn away. By giving little or nothing from our hearts, we begin the hardening process that leads to shutting down. We mistakenly think that by not giving we will avoid the possibility of pain if our gifts are not well received.

At all costs we must remain open.

By giving (loving) in times of scarcity, we are restored to a place of plenty. We not only receive in the measure in which we give, but with overflowing abundance. Give when you want to withhold, and maintain the open channels of your heart.

HEAVENLY PROTECTION

*He will command his angels concerning
you to guard you in all your ways.*

PSALM 91:11

A woman I admire at my church always prays, "May angels surround you, wingtip to wingtip."

From the first time I heard her pray, the imagery of that idea has stayed with me. I pray the same thing over my children, my friends, our house, our schools, over the plane when we fly, my car when we drive, etc.

I love the comfort and protection in thinking of powerful celestial agents guarding me and those I love. I can almost hear the rustling of feathers when I pray to be hemmed in by their collective wingspan.

Divine intervention is not luck, good timing, or a coincidence. It is His angels guarding us in all our ways. Praying in the name of Jesus evokes great power in the heavenlies. When you or others you intercede for need protection, He will command His angels to create a fortress for you. All you have to do is ask. Pray Psalm 91.

TAKE CARE IN WHAT YOU ASK FOR

*Give me wisdom and knowledge, that
I may lead this people.*

2 CHRONICLES 1:10

When God told Solomon he could request anything and it would be granted, Solomon asked of God unselfishly. He desired wisdom and knowledge to be a better leader. He could have asked for wealth or power or any trait or blessing to further his own greatness, but he did not. As a bonus, since God was so pleased with his unselfishness, He gave Solomon all kinds of extra goodies above and beyond wisdom and knowledge.

As I read this passage, it occurred to me that we could draw parallels in our own lives via intercessory prayer.

Instead of asking God to fill our endless streams of needs and desires, what if we tried simply praying for the needs and desires of others. Perhaps by lifting up other people before ourselves, God will bless our unselfishness as we slowly change our focus. As He did for Solomon, He will surely overfill our cups as we intercede for the cups of our brothers and sisters in faith to be filled.

Enough Is Enough

"That is enough," the Lord said. "Do not speak to me anymore about this matter."
DEUTERONOMY 3:26

"Mommy, can I have this toy? What about a pack of gum? I'm tired. Are we there yet? He hit me! She's not sharing! He called me a name. I don't want that one! I want the red one! Can I have a snack? But I don't like broccoli. I was here first. My turn!"

Just as I have limits on the amount of whining I can tolerate from my children, the Lord has limits with me.

After a while, whining begins to sound more like unbelief—which is a sin rather than just an annoyance.

The Lord has everything well in hand. He is currently working all things together for good on our behalf. If we could just trust Him instead of badgering Him, we would prove our faith and receive the peace He longs to give us.

When He tells us "enough is enough," it is time to get very quiet, very centered, and wait on Him to make things right.

BRAND-NEW ME

I baptize you with water for repentance.

MATTHEW 3:11

As a Catholic, I was baptized as a tiny infant in a traditional manner by a priest. It was an important moment in my spiritual journey, even though I was too young to appreciate it.

Later, as I came to know Christ more deeply, I had an amazing experience. One day during a very dark period of my life, I was awakened at around 5:00 a.m. I felt a very strong prompting to go outside, so I followed the urge. I walked out onto my back porch in my summer pajamas and was greeted by a soft, steady rain in the early, barely lit glow of dawn.

I stood there for a moment, sleepy and confused, until suddenly I understood. I got a big smile on my face and stepped out into the rain shower. I raised my hands as the rain coursed over me until I was soaked. It was the Lord, inviting me to my second baptism. This one was an experience of unparalleled significance.

I was new.

HEADING HOME

I will give them a heart to know me, that I am the Lord. They will be my people, and I will be their God, for they will return to me with all their heart.

JEREMIAH 24:7

Every single step forward on our spiritual journeys begins not with the foot, but with the heart. The heart is the true source of motivation, engaging the mind that urges the body forward. This is the essence of desire.

Of our own accord, left to our own devices, we have no momentum. We would continue to backslide and sidetrack into oblivion. The Lord knows this about us.

We must begin (many times) by praying to the Lord to refresh us and to give us a heart to know Him. He will increase our longing, heighten our spiritual desire, and arouse a godly passion that seems insatiable. He will call to us in a familiar voice, beckoning us back to where we belong and reminding us that we are His people. Our hearts will recognize His voice because we were created to know Him.

Like a weary traveler, we will finally buy a one-way ticket . . . returning to God with all our hearts. Home.

Personalizing His Promises

*I have suffered much; preserve my life, O Lord,
according to your word.*
PSALM 119:107

We can claim God's promises only by understanding what they are.

We must familiarize ourselves with God's Word on an intimate level. This way, whatever comes across our path, our first instinct is not to fear or doubt, but to claim one of God's promises to see us through.

When we incorporate Scripture into our prayer lives, speaking God's Word back to Him, our faith is strengthened and our power is increased.

Buy a blank notebook. When one of God's promises speaks to your heart, write it down. It won't take long to create a nice collection. The more you read them, the more personal they become. The more you pray them, the sooner they are revealed in your life.

God will restore your life. In all the ways you think you need it, and in intimate areas where you aren't even aware of your need.

PRAY TO OBEY

I will put my Spirit in you and move you to follow my decrees and be careful to keep my laws.

EZEKIEL 36:27

Disobedience is not a permanent trait or a personality quirk. It is a complete cop-out to say, "Oh well, that's just the way I am." Not good enough.

We were made in the image and likeness of Christ, so that is our standard of "good enough." Obviously we have much work to do. Where to begin?

We pray to God to set our hearts and spirits right. We pray to Him to reveal our obtuseness caused by our sin. We pray for an infilling of His Spirit within us to align our desires to match His. We cannot will ourselves to obedience—it's a question of submission, not of strength. It's a desire, not a demand. When we desire the Lord above all else, the strength to overcome is supplied by Him.

There is no temptation too strong for Him. We must submit our disobedience to Him or we don't stand a chance.

A Chance to Choose

Do not be misled: "Bad company
corrupts good character."
1 CORINTHIANS 15:33

During the time spent picking through the rubble, we have a blessed opportunity to "clean house." We can choose which things have value and are worth salvaging . . . and which things are not. This applies to material things, attitudes, and even to people and relationships.

One of the benefits in starting over is that we get to choose the new life we want to live. We get to make daily types of decisions, as well as grander, sweeping, philosophical choices. This is where the sorting comes in.

Are there people in your life who bring you down? Who corrupt your good mood and noble intentions? Who make you feel like you can't go on? Then it's time to say good-bye and take them to the garage sale of bad company.

Your new good life springs from your good character. Let's be purposeful and selective in the company we keep.

WHO DEFINES YOU?

*You were taught, with regard to your former
way of life, to put off your old self . . .
to be made new in the attitude of your minds.*

EPHESIANS 4:22–23

What didn't you like about the old you?

Were you too compliant? Too hesitant? Too naive? Too bossy? Too controlling? Too weak? Too regimented? Too rebellious? Too afraid? Too inhibited? Too critical? Too quick to settle for less? Too unfocused? Too indecisive? Too compliant? Too quiet? Too loud? Too inauthentic?

Guess what? You are invited by the Lord to shake off all the dust of the old you and reveal what He has been working on underneath. Like a renovation project covered in scaffolding and plastic, you now have your grand opening.

Open the doors, cut the ribbon . . . whatever feels good to you. The bottom line is that you don't forget to celebrate. You are not the sum of your old definition. You are not who anyone has told you you are. You are who God says you are. Your old self has been made new in the attitude of your mind, which is where big things begin.

Congratulations!

PRESSING FORWARD

Forgetting what is behind and straining
toward what is ahead . . .
PHILIPPIANS 3:13–14

❧

A cyclist breaking away from the peloton.
A horse pulling into the lead in the final lap.
A runner giving her last big push toward the finish line.

In these moments preceding a great victory, does a champion turn around and look back? No way! A champion presses on, hard, with everything she has. She isn't checking out the folks behind her. She is focused on giving all she has instead of worrying what others have to give. She is finishing her own best race.

Apply this spirit of sport and victory to your spiritual journey. Strain forward with all your strength. Do not look back; all that is behind you is over. Everything you need lies ahead. What others are doing is not important right now. What could have happened a few miles back is now irrelevant. All that matters is completing what you have to do, using the tools you have, and applying what you know . . . right now.

Stay strong. Stay focused.

LOVE BEYOND FEELINGS

Yet I hold this against you: You have
forsaken your first love.
REVELATION 2:4

The early stages of a relationship are so devoted, so exciting, so passionate, so consuming! We put our best foot forward and go to great lengths to get to know, and please, another person.

This elevated level, if it is passion based on "feelings" alone, cannot be sustained. Feelings are completely unreliable; they come and go with a whim and a mood. It is the difference between a high school crush and a ten-year marriage.

However, we all want to retain some element of this devotion, and the Lord is no exception. He wants us to reserve the firstfruits of our affection for Him. He wants us to love Him with the intensity of initial flame.

If this type of sustained love was missing in our failed marriages, we can learn how to give and receive it in our relationship with Christ. He will help us learn how to love with more than just our feelings.

ONE TRUE LOVE

Remain in my love.

JOHN 15:9

The love of Jesus is the only true unconditional and unchanging love.

Our relationships in this life can and will change, but if our primary requirements for love and hope are filled by the Lord, we will never wither or be disappointed.

Fill your heart with God and assume any other source of love is gravy—good but not necessary. In this way we do not place unrealistic expectations on people or relationships. We accept that we have been failed and that we fail others. We have total freedom in love, and give this gift to others. We control no one, and do not expect to be controlled. We offer forgiveness to everyone, and we live a forgiven life. We allow others to grow, and focus on our own growth in love.

The love of Jesus fills every void and is from an unlimited source. He invites us to remain in His embrace.

You Can't Rock the Rock

Jesus Christ is the same yesterday and today and forever.
HEBREWS 13:8

A natural repercussion of having your world rocked might be to fear change. When your spouse leaves, or you move to a different home, or you are forced to make a career change . . . all these things are mighty, and their effect is compounded when they occur in close succession.

Fear of change can be remedied by putting your trust and hope in the unchanging.

Jesus is the same yesterday, today, and forever.

He is our Rock. He is in the boat with us, calm and steady despite the turbulent seas. We can look forward to the future with unwavering confidence when we approach it from solid ground. We don't need to fear change when we know it cannot disturb the peace at our core. If the circumstances surrounding us are unsteady, we cannot waste our energy attempting to control them. But we can focus our efforts inside, allowing Christ to change and fortify us. We can work on our core, on our own personal steadiness. Perhaps we can't change where we are, but we can change how we respond while we are here.

LIVING IN TRUTH

*Now go; I will help you speak and will
teach you what to say.*

EXODUS 4:12

We are all hesitant, neglectful even, to speak the truth from our hearts. This lack of authenticity, often disguised as a desire to be pleasing, undermines our marriages, friendships, work, and family relationships.

God created us to be true to Him, and therefore true to ourselves as a by-product.

We may hesitate to speak up because we think that words will fail us. This Scripture tells us otherwise. Moses was trying to convince God that he was not the best choice to lead the people. He said, "I am slow of speech and tongue." To which God replied, "I will help you speak and will teach you what to say."

And He will.

God will empower us to glorify Him by living, and speaking, in truth.

SAFETY IN NUMBERS

*For where two or three come together in
my name, there am I with them.*
MATTHEW 18:20

We all need praying friends, not just playing friends.

There is no greater motivation than this Scripture to convince me to pray with my friends.

When we get together, regardless of where we are or what we are doing, the strongest tie between us is Jesus. Since He is central to our relationships, we are blessed by His presence every time we are in one another's company. Whether we are blessing a meal, praying before a run, laying hands on one another for healing, or interceding for our children, He is present. When we are active in an ordinary moment, the moment becomes spiritual simply by virtue of our company. We are not alone when we are together.

We feel the quiet strength when He joins us and the peace and confidence that flow among us, knowing our prayers have been heard.

Choose to spend time with those who invite His company.

RESERVING FIRST PLACE

*Bring the best of the firstfruits of your soil
to the house of the Lord your God.*

EXODUS 34:26

My most alert, most open, most productive, and most intellectual time of the day is in the morning. This is why I start my day with quiet time with the Lord.

He doesn't want, or deserve, our leftovers. Although this Scripture speaks about our material offerings, I think it applies to our other priorities as well.

The One who gives us life everlasting should rightly receive the best of what we have to offer. He should receive the whole of our hearts in worship. He should be the first person we talk to every day, and in every situation. He should receive our first and loudest, "Thank You!" when anything goes our way.

And in consideration of our daily work, our finest efforts and primary goal should be in pleasing and glorifying God in everything.

CAN'T GO ALONE

*You saw how the Lord your God carried you,
as a father carries his son, all the way you
went until you reached this place.*

DEUTERONOMY 1:31

Like in the famous poem "Footprints" which describes one set of footprints in the sand, the Lord carries us through life's rough patches.

My heart broke and my life tumbled down around me on February 8, 2003. I can honestly say that the Lord has carried me since that day. I reached a critical state of brokenness where I finally cried out to God that I could not go one more step on my own. I think God waits for that place of dependence, and from there He is able to do amazing things.

Let Him pick you up, dust you off, and carry you. Allow for one set of prints in the sand. Realize that He can do it so much better than we can. He will carry you all the way to the other side, setting you down tenderly and safely on solid ground.

Here and Now, Then and Always

I stand in awe of your deeds, O Lord. Renew
them in our day, in our time make them known.

HABAKKUK 3:2

Jesus' power is not limited to the brief years of His life span on earth. He did remarkable deeds of healing, multiplied loaves and fishes to feed the masses, and brought people back to life.

If anything, now from His heavenly perspective, He has even greater power. He has no further limitations of the flesh, and can be in all places at once. At the right hand of God, Jesus sees everything from above and has command over the entire universe. He can intercede for us now, pleading our case with the Holy Spirit before God. He will heal us the same way He cured people of afflictions many years ago.

Read the Gospels and refamiliarize yourself with His awesome deeds. Pray to the Lord to reveal Himself and His power to you now, in your daily circumstance. His hand is even more mighty, and His reach is greater than ever.

We stand in awe of You, O Lord.

No Excuses

A new command I give you: Love one another.
JOHN 13:34

Notice there are no caveats or conditions on this new commandment.

Jesus did NOT say:

Love each other when your relationship is new and fresh.

Love each other when you are healthy.

Love each other only when you feel like it.

Love each other unless you get bored.

Love each other until something more important comes up.

Love each other until times get tough.

Love each other until you find someone better.

Love each other until your relationship ends.

No, He simply commands, Love each other. Period. This means we are to keep on loving—when we are hurt, betrayed, tired, bored, sick, or even . . . divorced.

Love has no caveats or conditions. Loving the lovable is easy, but it is not all we are called to do. Obedience insists that we love in the face of dismay and disillusionment. Love intercedes for and supersedes all. How will you obey God and exhibit His love today?

HONOR HIS DWELLING PLACE

For God's temple is sacred, and you are that temple.
1 CORINTHIANS 3:17

Our bodies are the dwelling place of the Holy Spirit. Therefore, we must honor God with our bodies.

With so much emotional and spiritual revival going on during this time, we must not neglect our bodies. Our physical selves must be in balance with the progress made in other areas of our being.

We need to treat ourselves as holy dwelling places . . . sanctuaries. This means caring for ourselves to be worthy of the Holy Spirit.

We can all take stock and find areas for attention and improvement. We can better nourish and hydrate our bodies. We can get proper rest. We can improve our fitness. We can be mindful about our indulgences. We can choose to honor the Lord with the gift of sexuality by making godly choices.

We have a multitude of ways to improve the way we shelter the Holy Spirit of God.

RELIANCE

But this happened that we might not rely on ourselves but on God, who raises the dead.

2 CORINTHIANS 1:9

If you are of sound mind, and if you are generally a capable and competent person, you can probably rely on yourself to find a way from point A to point B. You might flounder a bit, but eventually you will get there. You might exhaust yourself, like a swimmer treading water, just to maintain your position. You may use all your strength just to stay afloat and not drown or drift off with the current.

Or you can approach things another way. You can rely on God's mighty power instead of our comparatively meager efforts. When we do things God's way, the current carries us to the destination He has in mind for us. Surely He, who has the power to raise the dead, has sufficient wisdom and means to handle the daily matters of our tiny existence.

How can we pretend to be in control when we don't even know where we're going?

Rely on God.

TRANSIENT TIMES

The Kingdom of God is near.

MARK 1:15

❧

How much better do we feel when we see the end to our present misery? When a tired runner sees the finish line, or when a traveling mother of three hears the captain announce the descent, we feel capable of enduring anything when we know it won't last forever.

No matter how bad things get, we can take heart that present times are only temporary. There is a great measure of comfort derived from the knowledge of eternal life. The suffering and disappointments of this earthly existence are so brief when seen in the context of eternity.

Every day and every step forward carries us that much closer to God's kingdom. When we can grasp at threads of comprehension of eternity, we can briefly imagine the relief of our own insignificance. We can rest in the relative meaninglessness of our current predicaments in contrast to God's power and His concept of time.

We are one day closer to Jesus' arrival. One day closer to relief from pain and suffering. One day closer to victory. One day closer to home.

A GIFT BEYOND MEASURE

I consider everything a loss compared to the surpassing greatness of knowing Christ Jesus my Lord.

PHILIPPIANS 3:8

Due to my path and pride, my faith came at a high price. In order for me to return to the state of being rightly related to God, I had to be stripped down. As a firstborn, straight-A-student type, I always strove to be perfect. And when I discovered I couldn't be perfect, I thought I could create the illusion of perfection. Then my marriage was gone, my family was dismantled, my reputation was stained, my dreams were mist. All the things that I had held in pride were gone. I was revealed as imperfect. I don't know if I was more grieved or relieved.

At the time, I didn't understand the transaction at hand. I didn't understand that sacrifice would be required. I didn't realize that humility had to be earned; I thought it was a trait you could acquire or assume. At the time I felt that my fees and penalties were exorbitant.

Now, with the gift of perspective being slowly revealed to me over time, I see that I paid in a meaningless currency for a priceless gift.

DEPART FROM DARKNESS

*Those who belong to Christ Jesus have crucified the
sinful nature with its passions and desires.*

GALATIANS 5:24

There is nothing as sweet as God's good company. There is nothing as rich as His generous blessing.

God does not depart or withhold. The only distance between us and His blessing is space created by our own sin. When we dishonor God with our poor choices (choosing to satisfy our selfish desires over pleasing Him), His anointing leaves us. This separation from God's blessing is the price we pay until we repent. Notice that He Himself does not leave us, because He promises not to forsake us. He simply waits for us to turn away from sin and turn toward Him. He is ever present, ever patient. He prefers to bless us, but He can do this only when we depart from darkness and return to the light.

We must work constantly to maintain our relationship with God. We must desire Him above all else and prove it by making the conscious decision to nail our sinful nature to the cross.

PRIDE IS EVERYONE'S PROBLEM

God opposes the proud but gives grace to the humble.
JAMES 4:6

Our tabloid culture is obsessed with the rise and fall of celebrities. The newsstands are full of periodicals that chronicle glamorous lives. The airwaves provide daily video reports of star-studded activities. But the media are also closely covering the scandals and failures of celebrities. Perhaps out of jealousy, the masses seem to enjoy watching the stars fall back to earth from their otherworldly existences. Why? Because we would prefer to focus on the shortcomings of others rather than look at our own.

We know that God is unimpressed with the celebrity culture that obsesses us, and He is equally unimpressed with our deflection of sin. It's not only the celebrities who must deal with rise and fall, pride and humility. In His eyes, we are all equal. Pride exists in all of us in equal measure, and God hates all pride equally. If we do not take heed to deflate our own egos, God will do it for us . . . and He will ensure it is a memorable experience. Impressions and expressions of greatness are to be reserved for God alone.

The most frightening symptom of pride is blindness to self and to the spiritual disease. We must pray constantly for humility and be accountable in managing our prideful nature.

A PROTECTIVE SEAL

Place me like a seal over your heart.

SONG OF SONGS 8:6

This verse brings several visuals to my mind. One image is that of a protective seal, like the sealant the dentist paints over my children's teeth to protect the enamel from damage or decay. Or the silicone caulk my handyman squeezed around the edges of the windows on my front door to seal out the rainwater that kept leaking in during rainstorms. Or the old-fashioned jar tops sealed with rubber rings that my grandmother uses when she makes strawberry-rhubarb jelly.

No matter the usage, a seal is a way to keep one thing in and other things out.

In this verse, Jesus asks us to place Him as a seal on our hearts. He wants to protect us by keeping the good thing in (His love) and keeping other things out (despair, discouragement, pity, heartache, fear, or bitterness). He wants to guard our hearts while we take sufficient time to heal.

Let Him.

When we are in despair, it seems that we are all alone. We allow our emotions to block the light of God's presence. But God is there in our darkest moments, and He can give us comfort and hope.

Great darkness precedes the rich light of revelation. Take courage in knowing that help is here.

LET HIM DECIDE

I know whom I have believed, and am convinced that he is able to guard what I have entrusted to him for that day.

2 TIMOTHY 1:12

❧

There is only one place, one source that can truly guard our hearts. Everyone we love will fail us at some point. We will fail ourselves. We will fail those we love. It is inevitable in this state of our frail humanity.

We have all been hurt or betrayed in this life, and to risk trusting and loving again seems insurmountable. But the greatest step we can make in this direction, before we are ever able to love well in this world, is to commit our hearts into the loving care of Jesus. He keeps His promises. He alone can be relied upon.

He is the only one worth entrusting the precious gift of our hearts.

If we remain in His will, and under the grace of His protection, then we know that when the time is right, when we are ready in the Lord's eyes, He will allow us to open our hearts "on that day" to an earthly man of His choosing.

A Disposable Society

"I hate divorce," says the Lord God of Israel.
MALACHI 2:16

We can definitely agree with God on this one!

God keeps His promises, and He intends for us to keep ours too. When we make a covenant before Him and break it, we are breaking faith . . . not only with our spouses, but also with God.

Society tells us to throw away the old and buy new, to abandon when it gets tough. God tells us to revere and persevere. *Have you done everything possible?* If you have, then the case rests in God's hands. The end of this verse goes on to say, "So guard yourself in your spirit, and do not break faith."

Cling to God now. Know that He hates what you are going through even more than you do. Do not break faith. He will work all things together for good. He makes all things beautiful in His time. He will not leave you or forsake you. His thoughts are higher than ours. Rest in His promises.

No Substitute

The peace of God, which transcends all understanding,
will guard your hearts and minds in Christ Jesus.

PHILIPPIANS 4:7

The unlimited, indefinable peace of God does not come to us via our own effort. We cannot relax or meditate ourselves into the depths of this peace. We cannot mandate it by managing our circumstances. We cannot will it by virtue of sheer desire. We cannot think our way into it with our intellect. We cannot orchestrate it with our vast skills. We cannot obtain it with our finances. We cannot force it by wielding our power. We cannot steal it from anyone's possession.

This peace is most evident when everything is falling around you, and yet you have a sure and steady stillness at your core. In the chaos you have more clarity than in so-called ordinary times. When everything is moving, it becomes easy to focus on the one thing that remains unshakable.

When you finally recognize peace as the presence of Christ, you will never want anything else again.

BEYOND OUR SIGHT

We live by faith, not by sight.

2 CORINTHIANS 5:7

This does not come easily or naturally to us. Living by faith is a spiritual discipline, and as such it requires constant training.

It is no small effort to learn to "let go of appearances," to learn that our perception and our judgment are inherently flawed.

Any time my friend Ann received a cancer update (hers or her husband's) from the oncologist that was not positive or promising, she threw it in the fireplace and prayed as it burned. "We're not looking at that, we're not accepting that, we choose instead to look at You, Father. With You all things are possible." In the midst of the trial she gave her husband a present, a baby blanket intended to wrap and hold their future grandchildren. Ann does not give disappointment a foothold. She and her husband, Bob, are both cancer-free today, and have four grandchildren to snuggle. Praise God!

However bad things seem, we always have a choice to live by faith.

Persistent Prayer

*Yet because of the man's boldness he will get
up and give him as much as he needs.*

LUKE 11:8

We are told to pray constantly, with the goal in mind of maintaining a continuous dialogue with the Lord. A consistent prayer life breeds persistence, often requiring us to return to the well and make our petitions again and again.

This lesson in persistence is not because God is hard of hearing or because He needs to be reminded of our pleas. Consider the idea that a period of waiting for answered prayer has to do with us, not God. Perhaps we are not ready to receive the answer. Perhaps the inherent blessing eludes us because our level of understanding is not yet sufficient. Perhaps we have not completed the necessary work to pave the way for our gift to be delivered.

Regardless of the reasoning behind His delays, two things are certain: He always answers prayer, and His timing is always perfect. Our responsibility is to keep knocking.

THE HONOR OF INTERCESSION

*I urge you . . . to join me in my struggle
by praying to God for me.*

ROMANS 15:30

It can be said that there is no higher calling than that of intercessory prayer. Carrying another's burdens by pleading to God on his or her behalf is a supreme example of love and friendship. When we focus our petitions on someone besides ourselves, we are able to keep our problems in perspective. In putting ourselves last, God rewards our humility by working on our own needs.

In this way none of us have to struggle alone, because those who care for us offer a united front in prayer. Prayer is the force that unites us, by bringing us together and connecting us to God.

The next time you are awakened for "no reason," have someone "randomly" pop into your mind, or have the "sudden" urge to call someone, consider that it may be more than intuition or coincidence. It is very likely the prompting of the Holy Spirit, tapping on your conscience, urging you to intercede immediately for a certain soul.

TAKE YOUR TEMPERATURE

Because you are lukewarm—neither hot nor
cold—I am about to spit you out of my mouth.
REVELATION 3:16

Have you ever mistakenly sipped morning coffee in the afternoon? It isn't a latte and it isn't a frappuccino. It's blah.

Being spiritually lukewarm is more useless than being cold. The life of a wavering, mild Christian speaks nothing of consequence to unbelievers. Better to be utterly cold and turned off, so no one has any false expectations or deferred hope where you are concerned.

We all go through times of tepid Christianity. In order to heat our spiritual thermometer, we must recognize our need to spend more time in God's Word, more time in prayer and meditation. We need to refocus on the light in order to feel the warmth of his presence begin to reheat us.

If we feel spiritually chilled, it is not because God has withdrawn; it is because we have stepped into the shadows.

WHO CHOSE WHOM

*You did not choose me, but I chose you and appointed
you to go and bear fruit—fruit that will last. Then the
Father will give you whatever you ask in my name.*

JOHN 15:16

You do not feel this spiritual hunger and longing because
you have chosen to follow Jesus. To the contrary, you finally recognize your hunger for Jesus because *He chose you.* He
knew, long before you were ever born, that you were His.
He knew everything about you, everything you would do
and need in every phase of your life. Your status in Him is
something He has always known; it is only you who are just
now figuring out the depth and significance of His calling.

Over time it becomes apparent that apart from Him we
can do nothing. When we are in close relationship with
Christ, He appoints us to produce fruit . . . and we are
amazingly fruitful.

It is an awesome honor that our names are inscribed in
the Book of Life. We want to live up to that high standard
by living submitted and obedient lives. We want to bear
fruit that is abundantly representative of our chosen status.

Never forget who chose whom. It will keep humility
and gratitude at the forefront of your entire being.

MAINTAINING JOY

Blessed are those who have learned to acclaim you, who walk in the light of your presence, O Lord.

PSALM 89:15

The difference is visible, practically tangible, between two kinds of people . . . one type that seems constantly depressed and downtrodden by life's circumstances, and the other that seems unsinkable no matter what load they carry.

It isn't necessarily true that one has a substantially "easier" life than the other. In fact, an easy road has nothing to do with whether we travel in peace. Retaining our sense of joy and wonder is not a matter of happy times, it's a choice to live a life of peace—no matter what. I have learned that I can weather the storms by praising God in all circumstances. Our paths inevitably will lead us through hills and valleys, and we must listen for the joyful call to worship along the way.

The Lord calls us quietly and urges us gently to see the divine in the mundane. Let's pray that our ears will be tuned to His voice so that we may walk in His light.

ABUNDANT JOY

I have told you this so that my joy may be in
you and that your joy may be complete.

JOHN 15:11

The kind of overflowing joy Jesus refers to is not the kind of emotion we commonly know as "happiness."

Joy does not depend on circumstances, finances, relationships, or moods. Where happiness is rooted in this world, joy is rooted in the next. Is it any wonder, then, that so many people find emptiness and dissatisfaction in their quest for happiness? Or why so many people are discontented when they reach their worldly goal and are immediately onto "next"? Happiness is elusive; joy is eternal. We will remain restless until we understand the difference. We must focus our energy on the pursuit of joy, which flows from following God.

Once you find joy, it cannot be taken from you. No circumstances, finances, relationship, or mood can touch it. This joy is overflowing, richly sufficient, and divinely abundant as the excess spills out all around you.

Don't dream of being happy again; pray to tap into the joy of Jesus.

Sand in My Shoes

*Remember how the Lord your God led you all the
way in the desert . . . to humble you and to test
you in order to know what was in your heart.*

DEUTERONOMY 8:2

My time in the desert was so recent that I still have sand in
my shoes.

The Scripture above begins with an important word—
Remember. This is crucial to me because I never want to forget my time in the desert or the lessons revealed to me there.

Regardless of how lush the garden of life seems when we
leave the barren dust of the desert, I don't want to completely put the experience out of my mind or leave it entirely in
the past.

The lessons of humility and dependence are more profound than the beauty of the garden. Perhaps it is only
because of my time in the sand that I appreciate the lush
green meadows appearing in previously barren fields.

*Thank You, God, for testing me. Thank You for loving me
enough to want to know and purify what is in my heart.*

HEAVENLY TIMETABLE

Wisdom and power are his. He changes times and seasons.
DANIEL 2:20

The Lord knows what is best for every living thing. Underneath a winter blanket of snow, the earth finds respite. The ground rests, seeds germinate, and nutrients from the decay of autumn replenish the soil. And so the world remains, until the appointed time when the sun warms to melt the snow that waters the seeds that sprout up through the restored earth . . . spring.

Like all parts of creation, we have seasons too. Seasons of growth, pain, rest, joy, and decay. The duration of our seasons is divine, each preparing us for the next. The decomposition of one season fertilizes the following season, enriching us to meet whatever lies ahead. The order of our seasons cannot be altered or rushed.

With God's help, we can use the rubble of our old lives to propagate the new. We can move forward as softer, wiser, more compassionate women. Only God has the wisdom and the power to work all these elements together for good.

ETERNAL DESIRE

All man's efforts are for his mouth,
yet his appetite is never satisfied.

ECCLESIASTES 6:7

I love to spend time in Ecclesiastes. King Solomon speaks again and again about the meaninglessness of it all. He isn't being dismissive or flippant. His remarks are based on years of searching for happiness only to come up empty.

He explains that he has toiled hard in the hot sun to amass his fortune, and he has lived carelessly, giving in to passing pleasures . . . and in each case has ended up with the same feeling: that this too is meaningless.

If all our efforts or desires are based in the present, we will never be satisfied. We will be constantly refilling a vase with a big hole in the bottom.

When we begin to live more for the Lord and less for ourselves, we can derive true and lasting satisfaction in all things.

TAKE SHELTER

He who dwells in the shelter of the Most High
will rest in the shadow of the Almighty.

PSALM 91:1

I have used this particular image to breathe my way through some difficult hours. God is solid and steady and offers me a place to hide. I imagine a storm whining and whipping across the face of the cliff, while I am safely tucked away in the cleft of the rock. Waves crash beneath me, exploding surf and foam thunder against the base of the mountainside, the beach utterly engulfed by the angry, insatiable tide.

The protection of God is impermeable. It does not matter what is hurled against us by the world. No storm can upset the core of peace offered by the rock. If we dwell in His shelter (and where else would we really want to be?), He offers us rest. When things get to be too much, we all need a hiding place.

Practice this meditation so you can spiritually find shelter when you need it.

STAY ALERT

Woe to you who are complacent in Zion.
AMOS 6:1

There is a profound difference between complacency and contentment.

Contentment is a grateful state of fullness, brought about by an appreciation of what the Lord has done. It is deep knowledge that we know we are cared for. The fact that we are loved just as we are should give us the courage and confidence to become more.

Complacency is the acceptance of mediocrity as sufficient, with total disregard for what the Lord has done.

As Christians we are always supposed to be growing and maturing. We are not supposed to get stagnant or lukewarm in our faith. We are not to use rationalization or relativism as tools for making our sinful choices presentable to the eyes of the world. "Good enough" is often a far cry from "best." God calls us out of complacency; He wants us to be sharp and prepared. He wants to draw us further into contentment by challenging us to become the people He intended us to be.

Beware of complacency.

WATCH FOR HEALING RAYS

But for you who revere my name, the sun of
righteousness will rise with healing in its wings.
MALACHI 4:2

Times of trial or confusion are grim and cloudy. I remember long stretches of time with constantly cold hands and a chill I could not shake. I needed a jacket inside the grocery store, and I wore socks to sleep. Perhaps I was just worn down or existed mostly in an icy atmosphere of apprehension and anxiety. I felt thin and brittle, like a lone sparse tree exposed to the wind.

The more closely I aligned myself to God, the more I began to experience a spiritual and physical thaw. Like going for a walk in early spring, I was acutely and gratefully aware of the sunshine heating my back and shoulders. The healing rays of God's Son cut through my layer of frost and began to melt my heart. Because of this overcast period in my life, I have renewed appreciation for a beautiful day.

I eagerly accept the warm embrace of a loved one, no longer resisting the Lord's attempts to heal and love me deeply.

SAVORING EVERY SEASON

There is a time for everything . . . a time to tear down and a time to build, a time to weep and a time to laugh, a time to mourn and a time to dance.

ECCLESIASTES 3:1, 3–4

This speaks wisdom like the gravelly voice of a beloved grandmother. A matriarch of the family, made strong and weathered by the winds of time, can tell you about the inevitable ups and downs of life in a way that makes you want to cling to every word. It takes peace and experience to know that there is a time for everything, and that "'this too shall pass."

We learn more about ourselves, and the great depths of God's love for us, in the midst of changing times. Our good times are sweeter and we are more apt to savor them moment by moment, when we have lived through the bad times.

In the light of eternity, all our moments are brief . . . regardless of if they are moments of tears or laughter, grief or joy. When we get to a place where we savor them all, we know we are getting closer to God.

GLOWING IN THE SON

Those who look to him are radiant.

PSALM 34:5

What is it about you? You seem different somehow.

Did you cut your hair? Lose weight? Have some "work" done? Is that a new outfit? Something is different; I just can't put a finger on it yet.

Perhaps you have experienced this—if not, then be ready to hear it. There is no transformation more deep or mysterious than when the Holy Spirit takes up residence within and begins to shine through.

You are softer and lovelier than ever, yet you have never been stronger or more certain and direct. You are becoming an amalgam of all the facets of woman that God intended when He created Eve. A hard edge is nothing but brittle; it shatters when tapped or tested. Soft does not mean weak; a soft woman loves powerfully and lives peacefully.

Your eyes are focused upward and they catch and reflect the light.

You are, indeed, radiant.

Enjoyment for All Times

However many years a man may live,
let him enjoy them all.
ECCLESIASTES 11:8

Picture yourself as an old woman. Your hair is gray, your face is lined with knowledge, and your hands are knotted after years of work and love.

Think about the kind of woman you want to be at this point. What does your heart look like? What kind of energy do you give to others? Are you peaceful? Satisfied?

We don't know how many years we have. We have no guarantees of a long life with many years to make amends or to invite or express love.

I, for one, have no intention of looking back across the timeline of my life to see "blackout dates." Regardless of circumstance, I pray to find joy and be present in the living of my life. We honor God with our enjoyment, particularly when we find ways to nurture joy during times of low light.

What brings you enjoyment today?

Preparation

Get yourself ready!
JEREMIAH 1:17

What do you do before a big event or a special evening?

I take a little extra time to get ready. I am more selective about what I wear; I choose jewelry or other accessories with more than my usual cursory once-over. I actually look at myself in the mirror and try to make the most of what's there.

If I spend time like this on my appearance for a special occasion, how much more effort should I be putting into readying myself spiritually for the biggest occasion of all eternity?

We don't want to be caught or surprised on this day. We need to begin now, taking the necessary time and making the most of opportunities for growth that will prepare us for our ultimate destiny.

When the Lord comes for us, we want to be ready and waiting to meet Him.

A Seat at the Table

*He has filled the hungry with good things
but has sent the rich away empty.*

LUKE 1:53

God offers us life as a spiritual banquet, so many tastes and delights. When we are "hungry" (which can equate to humble or broken down), we recognize our need to be "fed." In this state, when we approach God at the table, He is happy to satisfy us.

When we are "rich" (which could be proud, full of ourselves), we are unable to recognize our own need. We are smug and self-satisfied, and think we are in control and therefore responsible for our seemingly good fortune.

In this state, we may not even think to approach God's table. But if we do, we are not fit to join Him, and we are sent away. It is good to be weak. It is good to have our pride broken; it is good to know what it feels like to be hungry. When we are face-to-face with our own poverty of spirit, it is at that point God can begin to nourish us.

ACCEPTING PROMISES

It is impossible for God to lie.

HEBREWS 6:18

The Bible is filled with promise after promise . . . promises of healing, redemption, protection, provision, joy, peace, fruitfulness, patience, endurance, courage, love, wisdom, and eternal life.

My childhood priest, Father Arnold Weber, once remarked how easy it is for us to believe bad news and how hard it is to believe good news. Accepting good news requires a renewing of the mind.

When we feel defeated we often think these incredible promises must not be intended for us. Surely God had someone far more special in mind to receive these amazing blessings . . . someone far more worthy and capable.

No.

God confirms these promises for all His children, not just some of them. He intends them for those we don't particularly like, and He intends them for us when we don't even like ourselves. He intends them for those who don't deserve them, which would be, incidentally, all of us. And for as difficult as it seems to believe, for as much as it appears to be too good to be true . . . always remember this: it is impossible for God to lie.

PRAY YOUR WAY OUT

Bring me any case too hard for you, and I will hear it.
DEUTERONOMY 1:17

I always prided myself on my self-sufficiency. No matter what came my way, I thought I could get through it by thinking my way out, or forcing my way out by sheer power of perseverance. As a young woman I never came up against anything that couldn't be fixed simply by trying harder.

Unfortunately, some things can't be fixed by working harder or loving more. Some cases are just too hard for us. My marriage was such a situation, and finally (after exhausting myself), I brought the case before God. I asked Him to hear me out and take it over.

And then I had to let it go.

I had to release the entire matter into His hands and let the verdict rest. Now, no matter what comes my way, I know what to do . . . I pray my way out. The Lord is the first call I make, not the last.

LISTEN AND BELIEVE

*As surely as you live . . . no one can turn to the right or
to the left from anything my lord the king says.*

2 SAMUEL 14:19

Or as the cliché goes . . . you can run but you can't hide.

Jesus did not mince words. He did not soften His message to make the truth more palatable. His words are the same yesterday, today, and always.

We are the ones who try to veer to the right or left to get out of the harsh light of His truth. We prefer to find a different angle rather than truly change our ways in the recesses of our deepest strongholds. We would rather rationalize our behavior than do the work it takes to alter it. When the Lord speaks to us, He finds many simultaneous ways to reach us . . . a message in a sermon, words from a godly friend, an unexpected letter, a solicitation, a delay. We can attribute His campaign to coincidence, or we can start putting the pieces together and listen and believe.

A priest, Monsignor Edward Jordan, said, "We must apply His truth with compassion and without compromise." The truth is the same in all light, from every angle. It does not change.

Will we?

Ribbit

*It is better to take refuge in the Lord than
to trust in man. It is better to take refuge in
the Lord than to trust in princes.*

PSALM 118:8–9

If frogs can turn into princes, then it makes sense that princes can turn into frogs.

I thought I was living a Cinderella story, complete with a handsome prince and a size 8 ½ glass slipper. I mistakenly put my trust into the wrong hands. If you are reading this devotional, you may have had a similar experience.

My biggest mistake was in trusting in myself. I thought I could do it on my own, thought I could make things perfect, thought that no one could fail me or I them, and most important, that I could not fail myself. I was wrong. My Cinderella story was flawed, not just because we failed each other, but because we failed to trust and turn to God. If princes can turn into frogs, then princesses can too.

Our only refuge is in the Lord. The only hands worth trusting completely are holy hands . . . the hands of God. When He has primary custody of your heart, you can safely and appropriately trust on earth.

THE LURE OF LIGHT

*You are my lamp, O Lord; the Lord turns
my darkness into light.*

2 SAMUEL 22:29

A lighthouse guides ships in the dark.

A searchlight locates survivors.

A night-light gives children courage at bedtime.

A flashlight helps you find candles in a storm.

A headlight illuminates a curvy road.

A stoplight directs traffic.

A spotlight directs attention.

A porch light welcomes us.

Firelight inspires romance.

Moonlight evokes mystery.

Light. It warms, guides, and comforts. It sets the mood and draws us closer. Have you ever looked at an outside light on a summer night? It is surrounded by hundreds of insects, buzzing around in a frenzy because they are so attracted to the light. When we recognize Jesus as the Light, we start to swarm closer as well. And when that light resides inside us, it starts a buzz among others who want to know what the fuss is all about. Is it any wonder we read that "God is light," "Let there be light," and "You are my lamp, O Lord."

Jesus is the Light of the World. When He calls you, you are irrevocably His.

Let His light transform you.

When We Are Ready

The Lord your God has enlarged your
territory as he promised you.
DEUTERONOMY 12:20

Enlarging your territory does not only mean things like a ruler taking over another country, getting a promotion at work, or buying a house on more acreage.

After the Lord has put us through the spiritual boot camp of our trials, He keeps His promise of enlarging our territory. He tests us first to know that we are qualified and ready for more. Just like a manager in the workplace, He is going to give the best assignments to the most qualified workers. Being qualified does not mean being perfect, being best, or knowing the most. Often we receive assignments when we are the most broken or uncertain, because God is able to work more profoundly with a humble soul.

Enlarged territory equates to a greater sphere of influence. When we are more spiritually mature and educated, we become more useful to God. He can put us in new situations and give us new assignments because we have passed previous tests and paid our dues.

Instead of begrudging the testing, look forward with excitement, knowing that bigger and better opportunities lie ahead.

TAKE YOUR TIME

Daughters of Jerusalem, I charge you . . .
Do not arouse or awaken love until it so desires.
SONG OF SONGS 2:7

Just like an infant cannot go from crawling to getting a driver's license, we cannot skip steps.

No new relationship will successfully heal you, gloss over inflicted wounds, or instantly clean up a mess by virtue of a false fresh start. Regardless of the temporary bliss, you will sooner or later end up back where you left off, faced again with your old stuff.

Do it right. Take your time. Complete the steps and allow the Lord sufficient time to grow you into the woman He intended. At the same time He is preparing the heart of a worthwhile suitor, so he is able to recognize you at the appointed time. He does not call us to be withholding or suspicious; instead He wants to be our filter so that in order to reach the treasure of our hearts, a man must first pass through Him.

These things cannot be feigned, cannot be rushed, and cannot be pursued. They will be given to you when you are ready and not a moment sooner.

Don't you want the real deal this time?

SOLO = SO LOW

I have the desire to do what is good,
but I cannot carry it out.
ROMANS 7:18

※

This honest confession of weakness precedes the godly sorrow that leads to repentance. The Holy Spirit convicts us on our deepest level when we act out or think thoughts that separate us from God.

This desire to do what is right (or what pleases God), combined with the frustrating truth that on our own we continue to fail, keeps us in a humble state where we learn of our needs to depend on Jesus.

Of our own power and our own will, we cannot resist temptation or avoid sin. We may be able to flee or resist for a brief time, but the enemy is very sly and eventually wears us down without God's help. The Lord is our fortress of protection against sin. Only by seeking Him, by abiding in Him, and by relying on Him are we able to utilize power far, far greater than our own and live the victorious lives that Christ died to give us.

EYES ON GLORY

*Those who live according to the sinful nature
have their minds set on what that nature desires;
but those who live in accordance with the Spirit
have their minds set on what the Spirit desires.*

ROMANS 8:5

If Paul were a Q&A columnist, this would be the answer to the question "If we all have a sinful nature, how do we get beyond it and do what is right and good?"

Paul does not deny the existence of our sinful nature; he shines it under a spotlight throughout several chapters in Romans. He acknowledges that nature and shows us a way beyond it. His advice is simple—focus on what you want to become. If we focus on our sinful desires, we will sin. If we focus on God, we won't. The less attention we pay to sin, and the more closely we walk with the Holy Spirit; we will align our desires to match His.

Just like you can't catch a ball if you aren't looking at it, we must keep our eyes on Jesus and block out other distractions.

CHOOSE CONTENTMENT

I have learned to be content whatever the circumstances.
PHILIPPIANS 4:11

We know that if we belong to Christ, all things must go through Him before they can touch us.

We know that:
- His ways are higher than our ways
- His thoughts are higher than our thoughts
- He works *all* things together for good.

Bearing these three things in mind, we can face anything. And not just face it, but learn to find peace within it, joy in the midst of it, and courage while staring whatever we fear right in the eyes.

Each of us is accounted for . . . as a person and as the sum of our circumstances. God is in all of it, and in all of us. He tells us *thousands* of times in the Bible that we should not fear. Being content is a choice to be made, not a whimsical intersection of circumstance and desire. We can rest in all of it, good and bad, knowing that everything is going according to plan . . . regardless of how things feel at the moment.

It's more important to know "Who" than to know "Why."

NOT IMMUNE TO SUFFERING

The Lord said to Satan, "Very well, then,
everything he has is in your hands, but on the
man himself do not lay a finger."
JOB 1:12

The testing of Job is a famous story of faith and submission. Job went to depths of loss and suffering that fortunately many of us will never know. Yet, through all of it, he never denied God.

It is interesting to see how Satan cannot touch us without the Lord's permission. It might make you wonder why He permits Satan to mess with us at all. Why does He allow us to be exposed to suffering?

The only way to answer that question is to look at our first and best example for everything—Jesus. If God permitted His very own Son to be tested in the desert, and eventually to suffer and die on the cross, we can deduce that ultimately love is behind all of it.

If Christ experienced suffering, why should we assume to be much different? We were, after all, created in His image.

POLLUTION

*See to it that no one takes you captive through
hollow and deceptive philosophy, which depends
on human tradition and the basic principles
of this world rather than on Christ.*

COLOSSIANS 2:8

We are supposed to be in the world, not of it.

An ancient Chinese proverb says, "If you want to know about water, don't ask a fish." Our culture is so ingrained and insidious that it often becomes too difficult to separate ourselves from the world around us. Similarly, it has become too easy to separate faith from our daily lives. We live in an incongruent state, knowing how we are called to live as Christians yet fully capable of settling for less based upon the world's standards.

This rationalization is a "hollow and deceptive philosophy." It is the very thing that causes us to accept a mediocre or good life, in place of the best life that God wants to give us.

We are all polluted by our own water. Commit yourself today to align yourself closer to Christ than to the culture around you.

Taste and See

*Like newborn babies, crave spiritual milk, so
that by it you may grow up in your salvation,
now that you have tasted that the Lord is good.*

1 PETER 2:2

There is no relationship on earth more pure or beautiful than that between a mother and a nursing infant. The mother gives of herself to nourish her beloved child. Breast milk is essential, protective and life-sustaining. It is the strongest nourishment in the mildest compound. It is perfectly created to provide everything needed, and it changes constantly to meet new requirements. Supply increases to meet demands for growth. It immunizes automatically in the presence of illness.

As we move beyond infancy, we still require such sustenance—in the form of spiritual milk, which is Scripture. We need it; we crave it, as it is the only way to satisfy all our needs. It is also the strongest nourishment. It also changes to meet new growth requirements. It also immunizes us against threats. It is always present and always life-giving. It is a generous gift.

Taste and see that the Lord is good. Begin to know what you need—the Word of God.

MASTERED BY GOD

A man is a slave to whatever has mastered him.

2 PETER 2:19

If your paycheck is your master, you are a slave to money.
If your relationship is your master, you are a slave to idolatry.
If public opinion is your master, you are a slave to pride.
If sin is your master, you are a slave to the enemy.

By not making a conscious decision to put Jesus first, we allow ourselves to be mastered improperly by default. By not choosing, our choice is made for us. When we are not aligned with Christ we are susceptible to fall for anything . . . and we will. If you have not literally asked the Lord to be in control of your life, do it in prayer today. Back it up by your actions in seeking Him first in all matters.

Take some time to carefully evaluate where your allegiance lies. Who or what gets the best you have to give? Are you living your true priorities? Be a slave to the only Master who always has the best in mind for you.

SPIRITUAL NOVICE

The fear of the Lord is the beginning of knowledge,
but fools despise wisdom and discipline.

PROVERBS 1:7

When the Lord sifts us like wheat, I wouldn't call the feeling "pleasant." A season of discipline is purifying and strengthening . . . yet brutal. I have seen T-shirts when running marathons that have a quote on the back: "Pain is weakness leaving your body." Being sifted is just that; it hurts at the time, yet later you marvel at how far the Lord has taken you. Once we see the power of the Lord, it is a natural response to fear His mighty hand. We can choose to fight Him, or have Him fight for us.

The fear of the Lord is real for me. I want to remember my discipline and the lessons I learned when I was sifted. By keeping these memories alive and close to the surface, I can be constantly reminded not only to love and praise the Lord, but also to maintain a healthy level of fear and respect for His might.

If this is the beginning of knowledge, then I am a beginner.

Thank You, Lord, for loving me enough that You want to educate me in Your ways.

PAY YOUR DUES

*Whatever you do, work at it with all your heart,
as working for the Lord, not for men.*
COLOSSIANS 3:23

The Lord is my boss.

He gives me reviews, critiques, promotions, and demotions. He provides my benefit plan and my health insurance. He can transfer me from place to place, change my responsibilities, and develop all my goals and objectives. I report to Him alone.

My tasks change often. Sometimes I am caring for my children, sometimes I am working as a writer, sometimes I am ministering to friends, family, or strangers. Sometimes I am doing things for my church.

While my tasks change, my essential job does not. I am instructed to do His work and be His hands and feet in whatever position He assigns me. When I am facing trials, it is often a good thing because He is preparing me to take on more responsibility, and I am paying my dues.

Work for the Lord in all you do.

LEAVE IT TO HIM

I will redeem you with an outstretched
arm and with mighty acts of judgment.
EXODUS 6:6

When you fight on behalf of yourself, what do you win? Even if you get what you think you so badly desire—what have you lost in the process? You could lose your faith, your patience, your cool, your self-respect, the respect of your family and friends, or your good reputation. Sometimes we mistakenly fight so hard only to later realize that the battle was not worth it.

How much better than to leave the battle to Christ? He will fight our fights and redeem us with His own mighty acts of judgment. He has His own rules and His own rationale. He knows our needs, even when they aren't aligned with our wants. He knows when to fight and when to yield, and we don't.

Let His outstretched arm encircle you and draw you lovingly to His side. Let Him handle this.

SLEEP TIGHT

When you lie down, you will not be afraid;
when you lie down, your sleep will be sweet.
PROVERBS 3:24

What is worse than insomnia? Those awful nights when you see every hour on the clock, toss and turn, and cannot seem to turn off your mind. This is compounded when one sleepless night leads to others, making for an emotionally unstable person who cannot think clearly. When you are hurting or grieving you may feel like your room is filled with dark spirits. Nights like that are some of the longest, loneliest hours in the world.

We must pray for God to protect and bless our sleep. Read Scripture before bed and allow time to unwind and pray. Ask the Lord to station His angels around you and guard your rest.

Ask Him to quiet your mind and soothe your restlessness. Ask Him to use sleep to refresh and restore you. Ask Him to take away your fear.

Ask Him to fulfill His promise: "When you lie down, your sleep will be sweet."

PLEASE COME

*God has poured out his love into our hearts
by the Holy Spirit, whom he has given us.*
ROMANS 5:5

A key component of attendance is *invitation.*

Think of this: God longs to demonstrate His love, His mercy, and His peace. It is essential to create a time in the morning for clarity and connection. Several minutes of worship can make the difference for your entire day, and each new day is the dawn of your future. Before your hectic schedule begins, reserve some minutes for your Creator.

Breathe and try to generate a spirit of gratitude. Invite the Holy Spirit to flow into you, to embody your form and inhabit your mind. The Holy Spirit is the breath of God's love. God longs to fill our hearts with His love. He intends for us to live in a state of awareness of His presence.

It doesn't take much time or effort to issue the invitation. An invitation is all He needs to remarkably transform your life with His love. Lord, open our hearts!

The Lord Is Your Confidence

Have no fear of sudden disaster or of the ruin that overtakes the wicked, for the Lord will be your confidence and will keep your foot from being snared.

PROVERBS 3:25–26

Are you the kind of woman who is always looking over her shoulder? Are you always waiting for the other shoe to drop? Or for the rug to be pulled out from under you? Or for everything to start tumbling down? Are you afraid to follow your dream and try something new? Are you afraid to ever trust again and experience another relationship?

This fear can only be quieted by faith. Listen to God's promise in Proverbs 3. He is telling us to trust Him and not to fear sudden disaster. He is telling us to believe Him when He tells us everything is going to be okay. He wants to be our confidence and our protection. He says He will keep our feet from being snared—this means He will prevent us from being slowed down, tricked, or tripped.

When God blesses us, we are encouraged to enjoy it and praise Him for it—not to waste our good times by worrying about what may happen next.

Dealing with It

The swift will not escape, the strong
will not muster their strength.

AMOS 2:14

We can become very agile and adept at running away from our problems. We try to flee from our pain, our past, and all our issues manifested in our circumstances. The problem is, we can't run or hide or push things away forever.

Eventually we will tire from all the running and hiding and have to slow down. And when we do, all of our junk will come rolling behind us, headed straight for us at top speed. All the time we've been fleeing, our junk has been snowballing right behind us, picking up size and momentum. If we aren't brave enough to face it when it's "small," it will run us over later.

Now is the time to stop and pray and begin to deal with your junk. Please hear me that for as fast and as strong as you are, you cannot keep this up much longer.

Ask God what to do next.

Not Consumed

*Moses saw that though the bush
was on fire it did not burn up.*

EXODUS 3:2

୨୧

This was a sign of God's presence—a burning bush that was not consumed.

Have you felt the heat of the Lord's purifying flame? It can be so incredibly hot that you are certain you will melt, burn, or die.

The fire is intended to burn away impurities of character and leave the best elements intact. So while the heat is intense, it does not consume you. The flames lick and leap, but you yourself are not burned.

When you experience this fire, be ready to hear God speak to you. If you recognize the heat for what it is, you won't be too afraid to miss the message. Just as Moses stared in awe at the bush on fire, God called out to him. God will call out to you, too. He is not intending to hurt you, but to heal you and empower you to do His work in the very near future.

TRACING THREADS

"Return to me, and I will return to you,"
says the LORD Almighty.

MALACHI 3:7

Sometimes it takes a very painful season to give us clarity, to help us find our way back to where we began, to trace the very threads of ourselves back to our core.

Do you ever feel lost? Do you ever think too much has happened; you are too far gone to find your way back into His fold? Try as you might, do you long for God's presence only to be met with silence?

Do you see a woman of peace and envy her restful spirit? Do you want to shake her and say, "Tell me! How? Where? Help me!"

God gives us simple instructions:

Return to Me, and I will return to you.

Go back to the beginning. Find out where you lost yourself, and where you left your faith. Pick back up there. He is waiting for you.

Sufficient for Today

Do not worry about tomorrow, for tomorrow will worry about itself. Each day has enough trouble of its own.
MATTHEW 6:34

When Paul asked God to remove his thorn, God replied, "My grace is sufficient for you." God was teaching Paul something, to increase his dependence and humility.

God offers us this same grace, just enough supply to get through each day, step-by-step with Him. Then the following day we must refill ourselves with the Spirit to have grace for that day; each day is newly sustained. When our independent spirit is replaced by a spirit of dependence, we can fully benefit from the power of God. Worry makes us weary because we are carrying the weight of concerns that we were never intended to bear.

When we get out ahead of ourselves, we immediately become overwhelmed and fearful. God did not intend for us to survive everything at once! He manages our trials expertly—supplying light for each step, strength for each moment.

Stay in the present.

RECOGNIZE OR RATIONALIZE?

You shall not murder.

EXODUS 20:13

୨ଛ

We can look at the Ten Commandments with a spirit of rationalization or a spirit of discernment.

When we look at them broadly and lightly, we can shrug and say, "I guess I'm not so bad." Or we can contemplate them and apply them to our unique situations and personalities.

It was my friend Peggy who brought this to my attention. She called me out of the blue one day and informed me that she was no longer going to yell at her children. I joked with her until I realized that she was serious. "I have been breaking the commandment 'Thou shall not kill,'" she said. *Really?* "Yes, every time I use that awful voice with my children I am literally killing their spirits, and I can't accept that. I won't yell anymore." And she hasn't.

Think about the sixth commandment and be truthful about murder. Are you killing anyone's spirit? Their hope? Their mood? Their enthusiasm?

Ask God for insight into His laws as they specifically relate to your life.

CENTER OF POWER

I pray that out of his glorious riches he may strengthen you with power through his Spirit in your inner being.

EPHESIANS 3:16

Just like the foundation determines the strength, longevity, and structural soundness of a building—our inner being is the basis of everything else we are and do.

Our inner being, or our core, is where our soul resides. If something is faulty here—we crack from the inside out. If we are clean and strong at the center, we remain entirely solid. If we skip the necessary work and focus only on how things appear on the outside, we will soon spend all our time bailing water.

Paul's prayer is one we need to offer for one another. We must ask the Holy Spirit to supply our core with His mighty power. When He heals us here, empowers us here, the figurative heat of our center radiates health, wholeness, and power to our entire being and beyond ourselves to touch others.

Pray for healing in your inner being. Pray this same healing prayer for your ex. May God bless you both.

REMOVING IDOLS

In the year that King Uzziah died, I saw the Lord.
ISAIAH 6:1

Too often it takes the removal of something or someone in order for us to see the Lord.

The reason for this is that many of us break the second commandment regarding idolatry. We mistakenly think that *idolatry* is a term from the past that refers to carving pagan gods or sacrificing barnyard animals. Nope, we don't get off that easy—idolatry is, unfortunately, alive and well in our present society. An idol is anything or anyone who takes the #1 spot in your life. This spot should be reserved for God and God alone. Idolatry is a sin, and we pay for it dearly.

Sometimes if we do not heed early or gentle correction, the Lord takes more drastic measures and simply removes the idols from our lives. This frees us from the bonds of idolatry and creates the necessary time and space for the proper realignment of our priorities.

Upon Closer Examination

You shall not steal.

EXODUS 20:15

We might think that if we don't hold up a bank, or a 7-Eleven, don't shoplift or pickpocket, we are in the clear.

Think again, and again.

Stealing is taking something that does not belong to you.

You can steal credit and remain silent. You can steal an idea and promote yourself. You can steal someone's love or affection with little or no intent to reciprocate. You can steal someone's time by beating around the bush. You can steal someone's sunshine by taking up too much space. You can steal someone's autonomy by deciding for them. You can steal someone's growth by reaping what they've sown. You can steal someone's peace by projecting your own fear.

You shall not steal.

Keeping a commandment is more than not doing the evil; it's about growing in the good. Think today about ways you can give instead of take. Replace something you have used. Offer a compliment. Extend a hand. Exalt God in a random act of kindness..

PERSPECTIVE SHIFT

Set your hearts on things above . . . set your
minds on things above, not on earthly things . . .
Your life is now hidden with Christ in God.

COLOSSIANS 3:1–3

This concept of an "eternal mind-set" totally changed the color of my days when I was feeling gray and lifeless. Sometimes just shifting our perspective is all it takes to see everything in a different light.

Tilt your head and heart upward to feel the warmth of God's presence. Although you are living on earth, you can focus your thoughts on things above. By shifting more into the spiritual and less into the natural, you gain clarity and peace.

We can make great strides in our capacity to understand how truly temporary this all is. We just need to remember that there is much more going on than what appears to be. There is a simultaneous spiritual explanation for everything we face, just as there is a spiritual antidote for everything that ails us. When we cannot change our circumstances; we can try to change our vision.

Hide yourself with Christ in God.

STANDING TALL ON YOUR KNEES

Humble yourselves before the Lord,
and he will lift you up.
JAMES 4:10

Like a seesaw, when we push to leverage ourselves up, the next thing we know we are on our way down. And like a child on a seesaw, on our own we can manage a series of ups and downs but we never really get anywhere. Better to prostrate oneself than to promote.

When we bow down to the Lord, we admit our weakness and claim our dependence, which gives God something substantial to work with. We need to allow God to lift us up instead of attempting to do it ourselves. Ours is a temporary high; His is a holy elevation.

Honor must be bestowed, not created. It is given in small installments as a reward for a life well lived. Bow down before the Lord. Tell Him how inept you are without Him. Allow Him to redeem and restore you as you are lifted up by His mighty right hand.

Spiritually Naked

*They hid from the Lord God among
the trees of the garden.*

GENESIS 3:8

God must have known right away that Adam and Eve were up to no good in the garden that day. How lame to try to hide from the Father of the universe!

Yet how often do we do the same thing today? We think somehow that a fig leaf will hide our spiritual nakedness.

Did you ever notice that very young children "hide" by closing their own eyes? They are so self-centric that they assume because they cannot see you, you cannot see them. Are we spiritual toddlers, playing the same game with God?

Do we think that if we close our eyes to our own sins, predicaments, or relativity that somehow, some way, He will not notice us?

He sees *everything*, so we might as well own up to it all in prayer. When we confess our weaknesses to Him, we ignite His mercy and invoke His power to become better.

THE FAVOR OF FEMININITY

The king was attracted to Esther more than to any
of the other women, and she won his favor and
approval . . . So he set a royal crown on her
head and made her queen.

ESTHER 2:17

Throughout history, lives have been changed through beauty and softness. Because King Xerxes so loved Esther, she was able to softly request her desires and in doing so, she exposed a fraudulent man (Haman) and saved her people (the Jews).

She did not become queen or accomplish this feat through force . . . she allured rather than attacked. We women often forget the power of our own femininity. We get things done differently because God made us special. If we exert ourselves as a man does, we accomplish only a small measure of what is possible. Our power is in our softness and our vulnerability—not our edge. Trying to protect ourselves by sharpening our edges is denying our own power and disabling the Lord's ability to transform. Our strength is in who we are, and whose we are.

Lord, open our eyes and our hearts to seeing and implementing our strength the way You intended.

ALLOW GOD TO PLACE YOU

Many who are first will be last, and the last first.

MARK 10:31

Our culture places so much emphasis on being first. We unattractively strive and push and fight for our spot. We are told, "Be the best," "Don't be a loser," and "Winning is everything." This is yet another fine example of our faith running in direct opposition to our society.

Because I moved thirteen times as a child, I got to see many different schools. I was a shy and bookish girl for most of my childhood, so I learned many things about people from observing. There are always people who seem to have it all. I remember watching the people in the "it" crowd and thinking how naturally and easily they took first place. It's hard to understand it when we are young, but God has a place reserved for all of us.

How much better to allow Him to place us, rather than to ungraciously vie for top spot. He can elevate us much higher when we stop struggling and relax into His arms.

A Searchlight for You

We have the word . . . and you will do well to pay attention to it, as to a light shining in a dark place.

2 PETER 1:19

A light shining in a dark place offers us our only way out.

God's Word is such a light, illuminating dark places within us, as well as dark periods in our lives. His light internally points out our sins and inconsistencies. He does not highlight them to embarrass us, but to prod us to wholeness and healing.

His external light shines upon our paths, making sense of the maze of circumstances. When we have wandered off track and have lost sight of His light, we must wait for it before proceeding.

The Word of God has all the answers. Pray for revelation, and He will draw you to passages with your instructions clearly explained. He highlights His love letters to us, whether we read them with our eyes or hear them in worship music or spoken in a sermon. He speaks them tenderly, leading us out of darkness.

A LIVING TESTIMONY

I have written to you briefly, encouraging you and testifying that this is the true grace of God. Stand fast in it.

1 PETER 5:12

Each one of us, right now, is living our way into our testimony. God is doing amazing work in all of our lives, giving us a great tale to tell that will glorify Him and inspire others to seek Him.

I am no different from you. Just because I am writing this book does not mean that I have any more answers or knowledge or have made fewer mistakes than anyone else. *Not at all!* This is not about me. My pain has only been a catalyst to connect us and bring us all closer to God. I want to encourage you in your faith journey so you will turn around and encourage someone else.

This truth is God's work, and all the promises in it are ours to embrace. God's grace is carrying us all. Let's pray that we stand fast in Him.

THE PLANNER IN ME

"Woe to the obstinate children," declares the Lord,
"to those who carry out plans that are not mine."
ISAIAH 30:1

❧

Every year in late December I have a date with my brother for us to make our New Year's resolutions together. They range from serious to frivolous and funny. It occurred to me that, fun as this annual session may be, it is inherently flawed.

Why do I make my lists *and then* ask the Lord to bless my plans? Shouldn't it be the other way around? Shouldn't I be praying, asking for guidance in my goal setting and wisdom in placing my priorities, and then make my plans? Or maybe I can evolve enough so that I can quit making my lists and plans entirely, and trust the Lord to reign in my life.

Lord, help me not to be an obstinate child. Help me to turn to You first, not last. I desire what You have in mind for me because I trust that You know best. Help me to quiet my spirit so I can clearly hear Your voice.

TRUE MOTIVATION

Christ's love compels us.
2 CORINTHIANS 5:14

Love was, is, and will continue to be the only true impetus for real and lasting change.

This is because profound change occurs on a heart level, not on a behavioral level. We can alter our actions in response to fear, pressure, or a desire to please—only to find ourselves eventually reverting back to our old ways. Love is the only motivation that matters for a pure start and the endurance to complete the work.

Christ's love compels us to seek positive change in alignment with His will. Once we know the depth of His love, we are compelled to do and be more, for Him, for ourselves and for those we love. He inspires us to grow into His image and act on His behalf.

Are you compelled to be a better mother? Friend? Sister? Daughter? Mentor? Employee? Wife? Ex-wife? Co-parent? Christian?

What is Christ compelling you to do today?

SOMETIMES YOU MUST HURT TO HEAL

Even if I caused you sorrow . . . I do not regret it . . . I see that my letter hurt you, but only for a little while.
2 CORINTHIANS 7:8

We often fear speaking the truth because we don't want to hurt someone. We don't want our words to cause them to feel badly about themselves.

When the truth is based in love and our intentions are pure, the resulting growth outweighs the temporary pain. If the Holy Spirit is encouraging us to speak from our hearts, we cannot ignore His prompting. We cannot interrupt timeless, holy cycles of sowing and reaping. We cannot be soft or lukewarm when God is telling us to be bold. We cannot condone by our silence. The truth maintains boundaries, and boundaries are required for love.

Our own shortsightedness inhibits our understanding of current requirements. We must trust God in order to see beyond today. We must not be afraid of pain, our own or others', or use pain as an excuse to avoid honesty.

Jesus' words are like a knife, and He offers no apology for the truth.

OVERCOMING DISOBEDIENCE

Obey me and do everything I command you, and you will be my people, and I will be your God.

JEREMIAH 11:4

I have areas of disobedience in my life. When I rationalize these areas by the world's standards, I feel okay about myself. When I think about these areas in the light of God's standards, I want to run off in the garden like Eve to hide my nakedness. Like Paul, I get frustrated because I find myself doing things that I wish I didn't want to do. I have motives with long threads that only the Lord can trace and untangle.

Despite my temptation to hide (which is a childish, pathetic desire since God sees everything about me, everywhere I go) and break my relationship with the Lord due to my shame; it is now that I need Him more than ever. I need His love and guidance even when I am displeasing to Him. Just like my own children need baths and meals even when I am on my last nerve with them, my Father does not leave me untended.

Love does not exist only when we are pleasing. Real love is unconditional.

If you, like me, have areas of disobedience, ask the Lord to trace your motives. Pray to Him to fill you with His Spirit and cleanse you from ungodly ways. He will meet you where you are.

UNCONDITIONAL LOVE

We are not withholding our affection from you . . .
As a fair exchange . . . open wide your hearts also.
2 CORINTHIANS 6:12–13

When we are hurt it is a common reaction to be withholding. Parenting books say the worst thing a parent can do is regress to a childlike state and punitively withhold affection in response to a child's behavior.

A child's heart grows properly when tended to with unconditional love. Affection does not depend on behavior, mood, or circumstance. Being pleasing does not equate to being lovable!

Imagine if Jesus took this approach and loved us only when we behaved perfectly. We would never, or rarely, experience His affection. Consequently, we would wither away.

Since Jesus is our example of how to love, we need to seek Him in every opportunity. We need to love others in accordance with His grace. He loves us according to His capacity, not to the degree of our merit. We must love others the same way, not by our standards but by His.

Open wide your heart.

Lifting the Veil

*We, who with unveiled faces all reflect the Lord's glory,
are being transformed into his likeness.*

2 CORINTHIANS 3:18

It is possible to live many years of our lives under a veil.

A veil is not merely an old-fashioned face covering. It is not something white reserved for a bride, or something black on a widow's hat. A veil is anything we hide behind . . . which then breaks our direct eye contact with God.

What do you hide behind? Think carefully and be honest.

Your reputation? Your children? Your friends? Your fear? Your perceived unworthiness? Your money or lack of it? Your past? Your mistakes? Your definition of yourself? Your pride? Your family? Your title at the office? Your image at church?

Coming to Christ is an unveiling. We have a chance to understand and expose the veil . . . to come out from behind the curtain of shame. Turn your unveiled face to the Son and let Him shine on you, transforming you into the radiant beauty as He sees you.

HELP MY UNBELIEF

You are not grumbling against us, but against the Lord.

EXODUS 16:8

Every time we whine, grumble, vent, complain, rage, or rampage, we are grieving God. It's not that He doesn't want to hear our grievances or that He can't take it. He can take all of it, and more. It's just the simple fact that repeated over time, grumbling turns sour and can even become something sinful . . . unbelief.

When we whine about our circumstances for too long, we are basically saying to God that we don't trust Him. We are telling Him that we don't think He can or will redeem us. Can you imagine how this hurts Him, when we know how deeply He loves us?

Our grumbling is not against one another, it is against Jesus. When you think of all He has done, how far He has carried us, and all the good He has planned for us in the future, we can come to only one conclusion: It's time to stop whining.

HE IS IN OUR MIDST

Those who feared the Lord talked with each other,
and the Lord listened and heard.
MALACHI 3:16

In my Bible study we have small groups, or prayer partners, for the purpose of accountability. Being 100 percent honest is a mandate. The final question when we get together is, "Have you been completely truthful, leaving nothing out?"

When we have areas in our lives that need work or have been strongholds in the past, our shame causes us to want to keep these areas out of sight in the dark. But sin breeds in darkness. Suddenly a perverse thought, left unchecked and unconfessed, becomes action, starting the downward spiral of sin. Having to check in regularly with people who know your stuff is humbling and sometimes harsh. But I would rather be corrected by them than fall into a trap. When they speak the truth to me, I know it comes from a place of love. They truly want me to live my best life.

Trustworthy, like-minded people can shed light on our weak areas—inhibiting sin and promoting healing. When believers speak together, God is present and listening.

MONITORING PRIDE

Now we call the arrogant blessed.

MALACHI 3:15

What is it about our society that leads us to revere selfish, single-minded people? We call them "determined" and admire their "power" and "success."

What they really are is arrogant, and beneath that, afraid. They are afraid of being *discovered* (as weak, fallible, imperfect, inconsistent, normal human beings). While our society rewards arrogance, God does not.

Arrogance is rooted in pride, and we would all do well to consistently and brutally manage our own pride. We need to ask our friends for reality checks and we need to pray for humility. Pride doesn't manifest itself only in an inflated sense of self; it can also manifest itself in an overly deflated sense of self. As if somehow our misery and weakness are profound and require special attention, sympathy, and pity. The only way to have a balanced perspective of ourselves, truly recognizing our strengths and weaknesses in equal measure, is by asking God to set us straight. This may require some pruning.

Arrogance says, "Look at me!" while faith says, "Look at God!"

RAYS THROUGH CLOUDS

*You turned my wailing into dancing; you
removed my sackcloth and clothed me with joy,
that my heart may sing to you and not be silent.*

PSALM 30:11–12

It begins quietly, this revolution of joy, with a steady rumbling growing inside and a gray haze lifting as light begins to break through.

At first, the mere absence of awful feels heavenly. Soon enough we are surprised to hear our own laughter, like our joy is an old friend passing by at the airport. *You seem familiar. Don't I know you?* Plod along long enough, and you eventually get a spring in your step. You put lipstick on at a stoplight and smile when you flip down the mirror. The radio plays all your favorite songs.

The absence of awful is not good enough for you. It was for freedom that Christ set us free, remember? When He heals you, He will stop at nothing short of joy.

It's happening. Crazy as it seems, for as much as you never thought it could happen . . .

You are getting your groove back.

Praise God!

LIGHT REPELS DARKNESS

Blessed are you when people insult you.
MATTHEW 5:11

Being insulted certainly doesn't feel like a blessing.

But then again, when people who don't agree with God oppose you, take it as a compliment. If your faith makes an unbeliever uncomfortable, you may be prodding them to reexamine their position. If they can't handle your peace, that is not your problem. If they are just plain unkind to you, stop throwing your pearls to swine and move on, knowing you are blessed for having tried.

Knowing what God thinks of us and where we stand with God is like a rain slicker between us and the world. Where God's Word has piercing accuracy and profound effect . . . the words of people may pelt against us but our skin is never soaked.

A raincoat makes you waterproof; God makes you worldproof.

A LIFETIME OF DELIVERANCE

We are confident that he will continue to deliver us.

2 CORINTHIANS 1:10

When we accept Jesus Christ as our Savior, we alter our spiritual identity and destiny. While this is a onetime occurrence, the actual working out of our salvation is a sustained effort over a lifetime.

Similarly, Jesus not only delivers us one time, out of a particular season or trial. He continues to deliver us, day after day, situation by situation, as we grow in our dependence on Him.

When I hit what I considered "rock bottom" a wise woman named Paula told me it was a cause for celebration. I was in a foul mood at the time, so I asked her why on earth I had any cause to celebrate. She smiled in her peaceful way and said, "Because no matter what happens next in your life, it will never be this bad again because from now on you will know what to do" (turn to God).

She was right. And we do have confidence that He will continue to deliver us.

Appreciation for All Times

When times are good, be happy; but when times are bad,
consider: God has made the one as well as the other.
ECCLESIASTES 7:14

Recently in my Bible study we were discussing how much easier it is to feel close to God during difficult times. We agreed that we feel a stronger prayer connection and a deeper desire for all things spiritual when we are hurting. What is wrong with this picture if God wants us to live joyful and peaceful lives?

Humility comes from knowing where we have been. And gratitude should be our first response to any blessing. If we maintain a humble and grateful heart, we should be equally close to God regardless of current circumstances.

This Scripture brought this point clearly home to me. When times are good, enjoy them with a grateful heart. When times are tough, seek God's guidance with a grateful heart. We can understand good times only in contrast to bad.

God creates them all, so we can have balance and appreciation.

LOOKING BACK TO MOVE AHEAD

This mystery has been revealed to me . . . so
that you . . . may know the interpretation and that
you may understand what went through your mind.

DANIEL 2:30

Through revelation from the Holy Spirit, Daniel was able to interpret the dream of King Nebuchadnezzar. This gift of understanding was revered and Daniel was given a place of honor in the kingdom.

The gift of insight is not only for Daniel. We too can ask the Lord for the gift of understanding. God speaks to us in many ways. He created dreams, symbols, and stories to engage our imaginations and stir His desires in us.

The keystone to God's voice may require an openness to examine our past. Are we willing to look back in order to move forward? Ask the Lord to journey with you through your past to apply His healing to areas left untended. As you begin to understand what you experienced before, you will be better able to translate what God is trying to tell you today.

THE END OF THE WORLD AS YOU KNOW IT

*And surely I am with you always,
to the very end of the age.*
MATTHEW 28:20

At first I interpreted this Scripture to mean that Jesus is with us until the earthly end times. Or perhaps it meant He promises to be waiting for us individually at the time of our death.

But now I understand it differently, perhaps in a more broad and consistent application. I went through a season when I was very much alive, yet felt as though my world was ending. In many ways, it was. And the Lord kept His promise to be with me always, even at the end of my world as I knew it. And you know what? I learned a big lesson about the fragility of it all, and I understand that my "world" may come to an "end" many more times before I die.

But the Lord will never leave me or forsake me. Whatever happens, He is with me—supporting me, pruning me, preparing me, teaching me, and reinventing me each time I pass from "one world" to the next.

FIRM FOOTING

The Sovereign Lord is my strength; he makes my feet like the feet of a deer, he enables me to go on the heights.

HABAKKUK 3:19

❧

The path we travel is not always clearly marked with stable footing. At times on our journeys we come to places where the route has eroded, sliding down the mountainside. We know we have a long way to go; looking up is imposing, looking down is terrifying, and the present path consists of loose rock and craggy outcroppings of malnourished trees.

When a relationship crumbles and we are in the process of building a new life, we are bound to traverse some treacherous trails.

In these sections we must stop and pray. Our own abilities will not carry us through such hazards. The Lord, however, can adapt us. He can set us on the best path and give us feet like a deer. Our clumsiness and trepidation can transform into graceful and certain footing. Our skills and our circumstances are minor factors when He is our guide.

We can traverse the mountain path without fear of falling because the sovereign Lord is our strength.

FILL UP TO FACE THE DAY

Finally, be strong in the Lord and in his mighty power.
EPHESIANS 6:10

This is a great Scripture to put by your door, where you keep your keys, or next to the phone if you are expecting a difficult phone call. You may be dressed with lipstick on and think you are ready to face your day, but you are not ready if you are not filled up with God's Word.

Since God has all authority, He legitimately has the final word. He tells us to be strong. Not of our own accord (which is impossible), but we are instructed to be strong in the Lord's mighty power (which is unlimited).

He will equip us with everything we need to successfully handle any situation. He will provide grace for each moment as we grow dependent upon His mightiness. We can cultivate our softer traits, while He provides the armor we need in the face of daily battles.

Make a note of this final word, and put it where you need it most.

ALMOST THERE

Be strong and take heart, all you who hope in the Lord.
PSALM 31:24

Be strong . . . Be brave. Cast fear aside. Know that the almighty God is fighting for you. Know your Lord, your convictions, and how to tap into unlimited courage and power. You are not who you think you are, or who anyone else thinks you are…you are who God says you are, and you are strong.

Take heart . . . Don't let pain shut you down. Take your heart, all the broken and discarded pieces, and offer them to the Lord. At any cost, choose to live with love. A closed heart is not worth fighting for. You have worked too hard to get this far. Work with God to see your healing all the way through.

Hope in the Lord . . . Put no stock in emotion, circumstances, or the chitchat of bystanders. Put all your hope and every single one of your dreams at the altar of the Lord. He makes all things new and all things possible. Any other counterfeit will fail you.

He will never fail you.

ALWAYS REMEMBER

Whenever the rainbow appears in the clouds, I will see it and remember the everlasting covenant between God and all living creatures of every kind on the earth.

GENESIS 9:16

A rainbow is a symbol of mercy.

It is more than a happy reminder of the holy calm after a storm. It is an arrestingly beautiful reminder of every single time in our lives when we did not get what we deserved—when we received blessing in place of punishment.

Perhaps the mythical pot of gold at the end of the rainbow is the fortune of forgiveness. It is a wealth of understanding to know that as we have been released, we now need to release others. Our debts have been canceled, and it's time we wipe our own ledgers clean. When we can begin to treat others the way God has treated us, we will spread the colorful rays of His mercy into the world.

Many times God could have leveled us with His wrath, and yet displayed His love and mercy instead. A rainbow is a signal to pause, a reminder to pray and praise, to breathe a sigh of relief and say out loud, "Thank You, God."

ONWARD

*See! The winter is past; the rains are over
and gone. Flowers appear on the earth; the
season of singing has come . . . Arise, come,
my darling; my beautiful one, come with me.*

SONG OF SONGS 2:11–13

Did you imagine twelve months ago that you would ever survive this past year? At the end of 2003 I burned my calendar and thanked God I was still pretty much in one piece.

Without winter there is no spring. Without rain there can be no flowers. Without mourning we have no appreciation for singing. Enjoy your life in contrast.

You are the Lord's darling; you are His beautiful one, His prize. Your heart matters more to Him than you could ever imagine. He has great things in store for you, oceans of blessings and overflowing love.

May you never forget this winter of the soul, but go forward with joy and purpose in the spirit of love.

May God bless you in abundance,

—Kristin Armstrong

For the Mighty One has done great things
for me—holy is his name.

LUKE 1:49

I write "Afterword" but then have to smile because there really isn't an afterward. *Happily Ever After,* or claiming our beautiful and healed life in Christ, is a journey.

And so far the journey has been fruitful. Since this book was released, I have had the opportunity to speak at churches and conferences, to participate in book signings, and to meet some pretty incredible people in all stages of brokenness and healing. I continue to grow and learn with every encounter. Thank you for trusting me with your stories and your prayer requests. I keep them in a binder and in my heart.

I am amazed at how meaningful relationships are to us, how much they define and empower us, and how much they can damage us when they fall apart. I am *more* amazed at how our relationship with God supersedes all others, how it defines us, empowers us, and how close we can draw to Him when other bonds fall apart.

The woman I was through my divorce and the woman I am today are the same DNA but with a heart vastly refined in Christ. Today I make different choices, I seek higher things, I trust harder than I try, I understand the importance of healthy boundaries, I relish my freedom, and my heart belongs to Christ. I can tell you that my relationship with my ex-husband, Lance, is beautiful as He makes all things beautiful in its time (Ecc. 3:11). Lance is a friend, a support, and a partner in parenting. Our relationship is marked by honesty and respect. This is a tribute to the power of God and the commitment of two people who still want to manifest and model unconditional love for their children, even in the face of brokenness. God has given me the provision and patience to be a single mom and has reconnected me with my love of writing and given me a career to glorify Him. He continues to show me love that surpasses knowledge and fill me to the measure of all the fullness of God (Eph. 3:19).

I tell you this because if you are reading this book in a very dark time in your life, I want to be the first to share the light. Jesus came to bind up the brokenhearted and proclaim freedom for the captive (Isa. 61:1). He will do all the things for you that He has done for me, and I pray for even greater redemption for you . . . for His glory and for your peace.

My heart and my prayers join you on your journey.

ACKNOWLEDGMENTS

I would like to thank the following people for the irreplaceable roles you have played in the completion of this book, and in my faith journey which led me to heed this call.

Thank you . . .

Rolf Zettersten and Meredith Pharaoh
of FaithWords, for believing in a new author.

David Willey, for the confidence
and venue to pursue my passion.

Ann, Paula, and Debbie, for that day.

Paige, for the unfathomable depth
of friendship in Christ.

My Bible Study Sisters: Paige, KT, Leticia, Cassie,
Jennifer, Dawn, Jena, Crystal, Shannon, and Kristi,
for the fortress of your friendship and prayers.

Seed and Saskia, for your steadiness and integrity.

Peggy, my forever friend, for always reminding
me of who I am in God's eyes.

Father Jordan and my friends at St. John Neumann
Catholic Church, especially CRHP teams 22, 23 and 24.

Father Arnold Weber, for holding a sign at a
crossroads and cementing the faith of my family.

Millie G., G&G, Mom, Dad, and Jon, for my past.

Luke, Grace and Bella, for my future.

God, for eternity.

NOTES

NOTES